Women and the
Future of the Family

The Kuyper Lecture Series

The annual Kuyper Lecture is presented by the Center for Public Justice in cooperation with leading institutions throughout the country. The lecture seeks to enlarge public understanding of three dynamics at work in the world today: the driving influence of competing religions in public life, the comprehensive claims of Jesus Christ on the world, and the strength of the Christian community's international bonds. The lecture is named in honor of Abraham Kuyper (1837–1920), a leading Dutch Christian statesman, theologian, educator, and journalist.

The Center for Public Justice is an independent, nonprofit organization that conducts public policy research and pursues civic education programs, such as the Kuyper Lecture, from the standpoint of a comprehensive Christian worldview. The Center's purpose is to serve God, advance justice, and transform public life. It carries out its mission by equipping citizens, developing leaders, and shaping policy.

Each book in the Kuyper Lecture series presents an annual Kuyper Lecture together with the responses given to it.

Books in the Kuyper Lecture Series

The Center for Public Justice
P.O. Box 48368
Washington, D.C. 20002
410-571-6300
www.cpjustice.org

Women and the Future of the Family

ELIZABETH FOX-GENOVESE

with responses by

Stanley J. Grenz

Mardi Keyes

Mary Stewart Van Leeuwen

edited by James W. Skillen and Michelle N. Voll

The
Center
for Public
Justice
SERVE GOD
ADVANCE JUSTICE
TRANSFORM PUBLIC LIFE

P.O. Box 48368
Washington, D.C. 20002

Baker Books
A Division of Baker Book House Co
Grand Rapids, Michigan 49516

Published by Baker Books
a division of Baker Book House Company
P.O. Box 6287, Grand Rapids, MI 49516-6287

Printed in the United States of America

Library of Congress Cataloging-in-Publication Data

Fox-Genovese, Elizabeth, 1941–
    Women and the future of the family / Elizabeth Fox-Genovese, with responses by Stanley J. Grenz, Mardi Keyes, Mary Stewart Van Leeuwen ; edited by James W. Skillen and Michelle N. Voll.
      p. cm.—(Kuyper lecture series)
    Includes bibliographical references.
    ISBN 0-8010-6339-6 (paper)
    1. Feminism—Religious aspects—Christianity. 2. Family—Religious aspects—Christianity. I. Skillen, James W. II. Voll, Michelle N. III. Title. IV. Series.
BT704.F69 2000
261.8'344—dc21   00-033731

For current information about all releases from Baker Book House, visit our web site:
                      http://www.bakerbooks.com

Contents

Foreword

James W. Skillen and Michelle N. Voll

One milestone of the twentieth century was the revolutionary transformation of the status of women. Almost every aspect of life has changed for American women. Most notable has been their entry into the workforce outside the home. A special CNN millennium compendium shows that in 1900 only eight hundred thousand wives were working compared to thirty-four million today. With increasing eco-

James W. Skillen (Ph.D., Duke University) is executive director of the Center for Public Justice. Previously he taught politics at Messiah, Gordon, and Dordt colleges. He is the author of several works, including *The Scattered Voice: Christians at Odds in the Public Square* (Grand Rapids: Zondervan, 1990) and *Recharging the American Experiment: Principled Pluralism for Genuine Civic Community* (Grand Rapids: Baker, 1994).

Michelle N. Voll has been the development director of the Center for Public Justice since 1996. She is the editor of the Center's newsletter, the *Civic Connection*. Ms. Voll holds a B.A. in communications from the University of California, San Diego. Previously, she worked for the ambassador of South Korea in Washington, D.C. She is a native of Germany, and her key interests are comparative politics, organizational development, work culture, and biblical equality for women and men.

nomic opportunities and pressures, more and more women and men now struggle to balance the often competing demands of work and family life.

Elizabeth Fox-Genovese, the Eléonore Raoul Professor of the Humanities at Emory University in Atlanta, applauds many of the changes that the women's movement and second-wave feminism have achieved for women in the United States. Yet she is deeply disturbed that these achievements have come at an exorbitantly high cost to families and children. This is the topic she chose to address on October 29, 1998, at the fourth annual Kuyper Lecture, sponsored by the Center for Public Justice in cooperation with Eastern College in St. Davids, Pennsylvania.

According to Fox-Genovese, women's standing today is closely related to a larger social transformation caused by the elevation of individual rights to the highest status in society. "Our obsessive preoccupation with equality between the sexes and with monitoring its progress or regress," she says, "is distracting us from the nature and magnitude of the social change that is engulfing us." She cites the lack of "a common or shared faith" and "a public agnosticism" as evidence of the loss of a moral code that can hold society together. The family, and particularly children, are the big losers. The mores that once sheltered women also protected children. She criticizes religious women in particular for relinquishing the virtues of service and self-sacrifice and embracing a spirituality that often conflicts with church teachings against abortion and in support of lifelong marriage.

By means of historical analysis, Fox-Genovese assesses economic, legal, and social forces that have contributed to the slow dissolution of the family as a corporate entity. She believes that the mounting number of divorces, out-of-wedlock births, and single-parent households indicates that the institutions of marriage and family are at high risk. According to feminist logic, the legalization of abortion has liberated the sexuality of women from the control of men. But Fox-Genovese's argument demonstrates how legalized abortion has also divested fathers of a strong stake in the family. Moreover, with children being reduced to the personal choice of women, children have been disconnected from any social institution. The availability of contraception and abortion also makes it difficult for a young woman or her parents to secure the promise of marriage in the case of pregnancy. And in the courts, Fox-Genovese asserts, the privacy of the individual has taken primacy over the rights and responsibilities of married couples and families.

To overcome the excesses of individualism, "a Christian understanding of sexual difference and human equality" must be brought to bear on our culture and institutions, according to Fox-Genovese. This is best accomplished by recognizing "the complementarity of women and men and their joint stewardship for children."

The three respondents to Fox-Genovese's essay all agree that the philosophy of radical individualism undermines the institutions of marriage and the family and is particularly detrimental to children. They disagree, however, with the Kuyper lecturer about some of her assumptions.

Stanley Grenz, professor of theology and ethics at Carey Theological College and Regent College in Vancouver, applauds Fox-Genovese for advocating the recovery of an ethic of self-sacrifice. However, he does not believe that such an ethic should have to be realized by women alone. Instead of elevating certain gender roles to a normative status, he calls for "more flexible understandings of role differentiation." While Fox-Genovese stresses that Galatians 3:28 and other New Testament passages do not relieve women of distinct responsibilities for family and children, Grenz emphasizes that Christian women and men share a new covenant by way of their unity in Christ. He contends that this covenant has far-reaching implications for the mutual, creative shaping of human relationships and institutions, making it possible to honor the family while at the same time respecting the multifaceted human dignity of women.

Mardi Keyes, who codirects L'Abri Fellowship with her husband in Southborough, Massachusetts, agrees with Fox-Genovese that biblical marriage is not a social contract but a lifelong covenant, requiring partners to make unequal sacrifices at times. She takes issue, however, with Fox-Genovese's argument, which seems to imply that there is a causal connection between "equality" and the reduction of marriage to a mere contract. In Christian marriage, equality is consistent with "wholehearted, 100-percent giving of each to the other throughout their lives." Both husband and wife are responsible for safeguarding their marriage. They have an equal responsibility to avoid adultery and divorce. "Ironically," says Keyes, "Christian sexual equality calls men to conform to women's 'traditional' virtue, in contrast to individualistic feminist equality, which gives women the right to be as promiscuous as men."

The Bible is strikingly silent about gender roles, says Keyes, who disagrees with Fox-Genovese's notion that motherhood—as "women's special vocation"—makes it more harmful for mothers than for fathers to work outside the home. She points to the overwhelming evidence that fathers' neglect of children or absence from the home contributes significantly to social problems.

Mary Stewart Van Leeuwen, professor of psychology and a resident scholar at the Center for Christian Women in Leadership at Eastern College, compares and contrasts Fox-Genovese's arguments with Abraham Kuyper's critique of individualism in the late nineteenth century. Kuyper had valuable insights into the distinct responsibilities and rights of institutions such as the family. An advocate of biblical justice, Kuyper clearly endorsed the advancement of women, including a limited role for women in public life. But he did not overcome the Victorian bourgeois prejudice of assigning women primarily to the domestic sphere.

While agreeing with Fox-Genovese's criticism of establishment feminists, Van Leeuwen sharply opposes her claim that Christians who support less compartmentalized gender roles have sold out to feminist individualism. She says, "The truth of the matter is that there is no single, clear understanding of sexual difference and equality that can be turned into a litmus test of Christian orthodoxy." Van Leeuwen then proceeds to introduce three public policy approaches to gender and family: partriarchal reaction, functional equality, and social partnership. She favors the social-partnership model, showing how it neither favors nor disadvantages the decisions married couples should remain free to make about the division of their domestic responsibilities and their work outside the home. In the end, says Van Leeuwen, the key question for all of us should be this: "How can we put children first, without putting women last, and without putting men on the sidelines?"

Professor Fox-Genovese and the three respondents challenge both mothers and fathers to take seriously their family responsibilities—for the sake of their children and for the benefit of one another, both inside and outside the home. They challenge all of us to undertake renewed reflection and action toward a comprehensive and coherent Christian vision of life in which women and men may flourish together as God's servants and stewards on earth.

1

The Signs of the Times

In Matthew 16:2–4, Jesus responds to the Pharisees' taunt that he show them a sign from heaven:

> When it is evening, ye say, "It will be fair weather: for the sky is red." And in the morning, "It will be foul weather to day: for the sky is red and lowring." O ye hypocrites, ye can discern the face of the sky; but can ye not discern the signs of the times? A wicked and adulterous generation seeketh after a sign; and there shall no sign be given unto it, but the sign of the prophet Jonas.

Today, as a people, we show no greater ability to interpret the signs of the times than the Pharisees did during Jesus' lifetime. Our problem does not lie in the paucity of interpretations: Interpretations we have in abundance. But like the Pharisees, we seem unable to shake the premises and practices that produced the signs in the first place. Consequently, our interpretations rarely challenge the status quo.

Teen Violence

In the spring of 1998, two young boys in Jonesboro, Arkansas, shocked the nation by shooting four young girls and their teacher. Few, if any, Americans doubted that four children dead, felled by two of their own schoolmates, ranked as a sign of the first order. Jonesboro was not the first—and presumably will not be the last—of the school shootings that are marking the twilight of the second millennium. In the words of Nadya Labi, reporting for *Time* magazine, the news from Jonesboro marked "a monstrous anomaly: a boundary had been crossed that should not have been." It was, Labi insisted, a "violation terrible enough" to rob the president of his sleep and "to cause parents all over America to wonder if they were doing enough to wall away their children from the bad angels that can steal into young souls to stifle the knowledge of good and evil."[1]

Labi's language bordered on the hyperbolic, but she correctly captured the quality of horror that gripped Americans who were searching for a way to think about causes and prevention. Jonesboro mocked standard explanations: The school was not in the inner city, and the eleven- and thirteen-year-old shooters were not poor. If such a violation could happen in Jonesboro, why could it not happen anywhere? Suddenly teen alienation, violence, and nihilism began to look like the rule rather than the exception, and adults scurried to find someone or something to blame. The too easy availability of firearms, including semiautomatic weapons, provided an easy target, as did the promiscuous violence of the media, especially television and films, and video games. Neither attempt to identify and regulate the villains of the tragedy made much headway. According to the current interpretations of the Supreme Court, the freedom to carry firearms and the freedom to produce violent and sexually explicit materials enjoy the protection of the Second and the First Amendment respectively. More to the point, both freedoms protect the interests of powerful political lobbies that represent vast economic interests. Notwithstanding a flurry of rhetoric, our political leaders have so far refrained from any action that would significantly curtail the economic freedom of major political contributors.

Who or What Is to Blame?

The ready availability of firearms and the proliferation of violent, sexually explicit materials offer an inviting target for outrage and blame, especially since they may be viewed as external agents. As dangerous emissaries from the outside world, guns and pornography play well as the evil angels or alien spirits that can infiltrate the private sphere of the family. The infiltration is all the more alarming in the case of the Internet, which reaches into the interstices of the family to claim children for its own purposes, and parents often do not suspect anything until it is too late. No wonder normally restrained people begin to see the influence of the Internet as analogous to the "possession" by witches or demons that worried parents in earlier times.

These "external" causes have wreaked more than enough damage, but in the end they do not explain enough. The broad dissemination of guns among young people has doubtless increased the probability that their confrontations will have deadly consequences, but we do not know if they are more likely than previous generations to engage in violent confrontations. Are we confronting a world in which young people have new instruments for playing out an old script, or a world in which they are following a new script? And, if the latter, how much is it shaped by the sex and violence with which so much of the media and Internet are inundated? During recent decades, tolerance of sexually explicit materials has risen dramatically. Explicit sexual representations and references abound in mainstream materials, whether print or celluloid. Even very young children may now be exposed to a bazaar of sexual practices, and the slightly older child may use the Internet to track down all imaginable—and unimaginable—forms of sexuality. American youth of all backgrounds are growing up amid this deluge, and it is difficult to doubt that it is shaping their sensibilities.

The public world of sex and violence has much to answer for; yet the focus on external causes has effectively forestalled close attention to the role of families. Surprisingly few publicly attribute the rash of young people's pathological behavior to the collapse of family life, much less to the tendency of mothers in particular to work outside the home. For good reason. Few are so lacking in charity as to condemn parents, especially a mother, for the rage or nihilism or despair of their children, although some would like to hold parents criminally liable for their children's criminal acts. Horrifying as the school shootings may be, there have not yet been enough of them to rank as a statistically significant trend. Perhaps the public has overreacted to events that should best be viewed as aberrant and, consequently, do not compel us to reform our society and culture.

Most commentators continue to avoid drawing direct connections between the aberrant behavior of children and the nature of family life, not least because a responsible connection is so difficult to draw. Any attempt to link school shootings to the nature of the family founders upon the shoals of our ignorance about the specifics of parents' behavior and the ways in which it affects different children. Even when we have a good psychological understanding of family dynamics, it remains difficult to evaluate their causative role. Do parents "cause" children's behavior, and, if so, are parents responsible for it? Such a question may merit attention within the individual microcosm of a specific family, but it contributes little to our understanding of social trends. Yet patterns of family structure, dynamics, and spirit do affect those social trends, which they also reflect. Thus, even while it is impossible to blame a child's family for his or her behavior, it is entirely appropriate to draw connections between prevailing types of families and prevailing patterns of behavior among children and youth.

2

The Rise of Individualism

Discussions about the contemporary family abound, and they normally pit conservatives, who tend to defend the "traditional" family, against liberals, who tend to embrace a multiplicity of "family" forms and relations. Some of these discussions focus on the ways in which family relations advantage or penalize children, but only a dwindling number of participants on either side has the temerity to insist that children would fare better if their mothers did not work outside the home, or, at least, if one of their parents were at home when the children return from school. These days only the most unreconstructed traditionalists—many with some hesitation—dare to suggest that a mother and a father may play different roles in a child's life and, hence, have different responsibilities. Indeed, notwithstanding currents of criticism from both the left and the right, our times manifest an astounding complacency toward the ominous tendencies of our political, social, and cultural life, for within a remarkably brief period we have, almost without noticing, embraced a cataclysmic transformation of the very nature of our society.

The Rise of the Individual

Today, Americans have endowed the liberation and the rights of the individual with a preeminence and sanctity that set us apart from virtually every other known society. Our unprecedented privileging of the individual has reduced the ties that bind us to society to a mere fiction—and a contested fiction at that. From a structural or anthropological perspective, human societies have originated and developed as communal enterprises devoted to production of adequate subsistence for their members and reproduction (or increase) of their population and culture. Throughout the world, growing social and economic complexity, notably in the form commonly known as modernization, has led societies to attribute greater independence to their individual members or, more commonly, to individual family units. Worldwide, the spread of capitalism has reinforced and sped the process of individuation, with the result that the idea of individual human rights is gaining wider currency in many countries.

The progress of capitalism and the ideology of individualism should not delude us into viewing the sanctity of the individual as a global norm, which it demonstrably is not. Throughout most of the world, individuals still depend heavily on kin for survival, and families still exercise considerable sway over their members. Traditional religions, most dramatically Islam, and strong states reinforce the primacy of group membership even when they do not always support the power of the family. Even a minimal sketch underscores how anomalous our emphasis on the rights of the individual looks in global and historical perspective. And a greater anomaly: Our complacent certainty assumes it to be an inviolable norm. Our complacency has dangerously blinded us to the truth of our situation, for what we insist on viewing as normative actually represents a revolution, the implications and magnitude of which we have not begun to fathom.

The Individual and Religion

As a small indication of those implications, we might briefly consider the preponderant cultural attitude toward and social standing of religion. Relying on a widespread misunderstanding of the First Amendment, we have rejected public worship on the grounds that it violates the freedom of the individual and the separation of church and state. We have, consequently, lost the sense of a common or shared faith, even in the general sense of the Judeo-Christian tradition. Respect for the diversity of religious belief may require such public agnosticism, but the cost is high, notably the loss of a generally binding code of right and wrong. Many commentators appear to take comfort in the evidence that Americans' interest in spirituality is flourishing, and so it is, in every conceivable guise from the Christian solidity of Eastern Orthodoxy to psychic readings and New Age cults of self-realization. A recent poll further demonstrates that American women are turning to religion in growing numbers.[1]

Thus, during the past two years, the number of American women who claim that religion plays an important role in their lives has increased sharply. Today, three-quarters see religion as important, and half would like religious organizations to participate in public discussion of men's and women's roles in society. Almost half would also like religious organizations to participate in the public discussion of abortion, and more than two-thirds favor restrictions on abortion.[2] These findings offer reasons for optimism about changes in our cultural climate, but they also present formidable problems of interpretation, for the very women who acknowledge the importance of religion in their lives, even those who doubt the wisdom of abortion on demand, do not seem to view their church's teachings on sexuality and men's and women's roles as authoritative. The problem is not simply that women find their priests, ministers, or rabbis reactionary or punitive concerning women's roles.

More than half the women who attend church believe that their clergy favors equality between women and men, and more than three-quarters claim that their clergy offers instruction on what it means to be a good mother and a good wife. The real problem seems to be that many church-going women do not acknowledge their church's teaching as influential, much less as binding, on their own lives.

A mere third of the women who value religion and attend church believe that their church has decisively influenced their view of abortion, less than a quarter credit religion with an important influence on their understanding of marriage, and only 13 percent credit it with influencing their understanding of gender equality. At the same time, a large majority claims that religion offers them moral and ethical standards (88 percent), helps them with personal problems (85 percent), makes them feel they belong to a community (84 percent), and offers them opportunities for leadership (75 percent). At first glance, these findings appear confusing. What are we to make of women who believe that their church offers them moral and ethical standards but who are not influenced by its teachings on abortion, marriage, or gender equality? It seems possible that women primarily value religion for assistance with personal problems, a sense of belonging, and the opportunity for leadership. If so, we might conclude that they value religion for what it offers them rather than for what it demands of them.

These findings bear a strong resemblance to those of James Davison Hunter and his associates.[3] In their survey, respondents consistently resisted the idea that moral imperatives should govern disparate situations. Time and again, they refused to hold someone else to a moral standard when they did not know her feelings about her situation. Both surveys suggest that even Americans who view themselves as religious or spiritual resist the idea of religion's authority over their lives. In other words, they believe that the ultimate religious judgment emanates from the individual rather than from God, much less from his priests, ministers, and rabbis. The emphasis on the private rein-forces individualism at the expense of the social bond, es-pecially with respect to the claims of morality, which is re-duced from God's commandment to a matter of personal preference or choice.[4] Yet no amount of private spirituality can substitute for public—that is, community—worship.

The Individual and the Family

Just as individualism has so permeated many Americans' views of religion as to transform its meaning, so has it permeated our understanding of the family as a unit and of the relations among its members. Throughout much of American history, the family ranked as a foundational social unit and was, as Alexis de Tocqueville noted in *Democracy in America,* essential to the well-being of the country. Throughout the nineteenth and much of the twentieth cen-tury, the family ranked as the main social institution and en-joyed a significant measure of autonomy. Especially in the slaveholding South and the frontier West, but also through-out the older northern states, the family represented a kind of corporate enclave. Even within the bustle of the compet-itive individualism, capitalism, and democracy that were coming to dominate the northeastern states, the family re-mained tied to hierarchical principles that placed the man, husband and father, in authority over all, including his wife, and placed both parents in authority over their children.

The special standing of the family had a long intellectual and political pedigree that had marked it as "different in kind" or "distinct" from other institutions or associations. Similarly, the law, following these traditions, had marked re-lations among family members and of family members with those outside the family as both discrete and unique. In other words, family members occupied particularistic posi-tions by virtue of their place within the family: They were husband, wife, father, mother, child rather than abstract individuals.[5] In theory, particularism promised that each member of the family could be excellent—or flawed—according to the standards of his or her specific role rather than in the abstract. By the same token, particularism undercut any claims to assess the relations among family members according to the standards of abstract individual right.

Women as Individuals

The first stirrings of the women's movement in the mid-nineteenth century inaugurated a long and ultimately successful campaign against the injustice of the subordination of women to men within the family. These early women's rights activists, frequently evoking an analogy between the condition of married women and that of slaves, gradually secured a number of reforms, beginning with a married woman's right to own property in her own name. From the start, the most radical of them insisted on the importance of winning for women full standing as individuals, independent of their family relations. Second-wave feminists even more sharply condemned the family as the cradle of women's oppression, and they successfully campaigned for no-fault divorce, recognition of marital rape, and other forms of assistance for the wives of abusive husbands.

Many of these changes represented significant progress for women, and few today would, I think, dispute their positive value, but there is also reason to believe that they have come at an exorbitantly high price. Their impact has been all the greater because they occurred in conjunction with—and arguably partially because of—a massive movement of married women and mothers of small children into the labor force. Thus, just as the formal bonds of the family were being weakened by legal reforms, the presence of women in the family was decreasing because of the time they were spending at work, and women's economic independence from their husbands was increasing because of the wages they were earning. Arguably, the most serious casualties of this slow dissolution of the family's corporate character are the children, who are increasingly being turned over to others or left to their own devices. Taken as a whole, these developments represent a massive infusion of individualist principles and practices into the family and the attendant destruction of the notion of the privacy right of the family qua family—or the family as a corporate body rather than an arbitrary collection of individuals.[6] Many contemporary commentators have celebrated these trends, arguing that "a family based privacy right is out of sync with contemporary sociological reality," that "a family-based privacy right is both constitutionally and philosophically unsound," and that the notion of familial privacy should give way to a notion of privacy that "centers on autonomous individuals."[7]

Heated struggle over the rights, nature, and mission of women has marked the recent decades during which the most dramatic of these changes have occurred. Within religious as well as secular circles, these changes have generated intense and often polarizing struggles between those who demand the "liberation" of women from unjust constraints and those who enjoin women to reembrace their "traditional" roles and responsibilities. In practice, most women have rejected both extremes, preferring to adopt aspects of each in the hope of finding a livable balance between a measure of individual freedom for themselves and attention to their obligations and responsibilities to others. The ability of women to get on with their lives in the midst of this raging rhetorical battle might seem to suggest that the clash of opinions can be dismissed as much ado about nothing, but before we settle for that comfortable agnosticism, we should recall that the extremists exercise considerable influence on both public opinion and policy.

Angry charges from both camps abound, while none of us can confidently assess the upheaval through which we are living. Nor can we determine the measure to which the transformation of the situation of women has caused the up-heaval and the measure to which it is another by-product of larger social trends. Or to put it differently, in what measure have women struggled to improve their standing as individ-uals because traditional structures are collapsing, and in what measure have their struggles accelerated, or even caused, the collapse? Doubtless, some of each, although the allocation of blame serves no useful purpose. The rhetorical battles have distracted us from the most significant aspects of the change, for independent of whether one approves the new pattern of women's lives, it is difficult to deny that the crevice that has opened between the lives of women and the nurturing stewardship of families and children has already had crippling consequences and portends even worse ones.

One thing is blindingly clear: The transformation of women's lives and expectations during recent decades has no historical precedent, and its consequences reach into every aspect of family and societal life. Above all, the changes in women's lives and expectations are having a radical im-pact on families and the very idea of the family, and there-fore on the lives of children, and therefore on the character and prospects of future generations. Women are the bridges across which change passes between the individual and the world, and, these days, between the world and the individ-ual. Fathers, too, transmit change in the world into the inte-rior life of families, and we know that their contribution to children's lives is indispensable. But in our time, the change in women's public lives is proving decisively more significant and influential—although not exclusively in positive ways.

3

Feminism and the Struggle for Equality

One of second-wave feminism's great contributions was to encourage us to look at the family and society through women's eyes—to focus on and privilege the story of the individual woman. From this perspective, many social relations and institutions, notably the family, began to look a little suspect. It did not take much consciousness-raising to show women that they were performing a disproportionate share of household and child-rearing labor, especially since they had known it all along. But consciousness-raising and other feminist efforts did teach many to view their contributions to family life in a new—and not entirely favorable—way. Even those who were not predisposed to regard the family as the cradle of women's oppression were often inclined to chafe at the unequal distribution of domestic labor between women and men. Women's steadily increasing participation in the labor force resulted in a growing resemblance between their nondomestic lives and those of their husbands, but it did not inevitably result in their husbands' assuming a larger share of the burden at home.[1] And what was true with regard to the division of domestic labor also proved true in many other spheres of life as well. Justice required that women enjoy equality with men in all spheres of life. The precise meaning of equality, however, which could refer to opportunity or results, remained elusive and variable according to the situation, but the ideal has acquired iconic standing. ⤚

At one level, the promotion of equality between women and men appeared natural and overdue. Why should girls not attend Harvard, Yale, and Princeton like their brothers? Why should they not enjoy access to professional schools in proportion to their talents and, thereafter, equal access to the professions and equal pay for equal work? Equality in the public world of education, employment, sports, politics, and earnings gained broad acceptance in a remarkably brief span of time. By the early 1990s, women were attending colleges and universities in equal or greater numbers than men, they were steadily increasing their representation in graduate and professional schools, and they were entering the jobs and professions for which they were prepared. Most dramatically, virtually across the employment spectrum—from McDonald's to Wall Street—entry-level women were earning the same pay as entry-level men.

Notwithstanding rapid progress, many feminists have found this growing equality between women and men in the public sphere less than satisfactory. By any objective criterion, the comparative improvement in the position of women relative to that of men has been revolutionary, vastly surpassing the improvement secured in a comparable span of time by any other working group in history. But it has yet to produce equal representation of women and men in the most prestigious and lucrative positions. Perhaps more important, the evidence suggests that most women are still unlikely to pursue careers with as much single-minded dedication as men. Consequently, women are still less likely than men to break into the highest echelons—to crack the glass ceiling—of business, the professions, and politics. In practice, these patterns testify to the persisting inclination of women to devote more time than men to family and children. But feminists do not readily countenance the possibility that women, in devoting more time than men to family and children, are expressing a preference. Many also find evidence of persisting discrimination in the tendency of women and men to adopt a somewhat different balance between domestic and public responsibilities, although overt institutional discrimination is becoming increasingly rare. Some continue to insist that hiring and promotion require more aggressive oversight and intervention; others focus on the need to make men carry an equal share of domestic and familial responsibilities.

Here, I have no interest in debating the specifics of these strategies, although I doubt the long-range value of either. In the interest of refocusing the discussion, I will concede that neither the public nor the domestic world is invariably fair and that men may, in any given instance, continue to enjoy an unfair advantage over women, just as some women may enjoy an unfair advantage over men. Nothing is more self-evident than the tendency of different economic, political, and ideological systems to advantage different social groups: Warriors did well under feudalism, entrepreneurs did well under capitalism, and so forth. Today, our obsessive preoccupation with equality between the sexes and with monitoring its progress or regress is distracting us from the nature and magnitude of the social change that is engulfing us. Since the situation of women lies at the core of this change, women have understandably tended to perceive it subjectively as a function of their personal experience, and their subjective perceptions have effectively masked the larger underlying patterns.

Sexual Liberation and Its Influence on the Family

Take the case of sexual liberation. From the early phases of second-wave feminism, the sexual liberation of women ranked as a major objective. For many feminists, *Roe v Wade* (1973) figured as the charter of the true freedom of women as individuals. According to this logic, the legalization of abortion liberated women's sexuality from the control of men. Finally free to control their own reproductive abilities by *not* having children, women would be as free as men to enjoy their own sexuality. If you credit feminists, legal abortion liberated female sexuality from the centuries-long domination of men. The freedom to enjoy sex at will and without fear of the consequences promoted women to sexual adulthood and autonomy. Defense of abortion on demand has remained a sacred tenet of feminists, who regard it as the cornerstone of women's sexual freedom and who oppose any restrictions on it. In this spirit, feminists campaign against parental consent for minors, spousal consent or notification for wives, a twenty-four- or forty-eight-hour waiting period between the decision and the abortion, or restrictions on late-term or partial birth abortions.

Feminist campaigns to secure the legal standing of women as sexually autonomous beings have had dramatic consequences for the social and legal standing of the family. A woman's right to abortion has been defended in political language as an individual right—a woman's right to sexual freedom. No less significantly, it has been defended on the grounds of privacy. Consider the implications of these two positions. In the first instance, a woman has a right to be liberated from children—the possible consequence of her sexuality. This strategy effectively divorces children from any social institution by labeling them the concern of a woman rather than of a woman and a man. The second argument points in the same direction by reducing privacy to the privacy of the individual rather than the privacy of the couple or the family. As Mary Ann Glendon has argued, this interpretation of the right of privacy is a radical innovation in American law, and it represents a significant departure from the legal norms of Western European nations. Symbolically, the reduction of privacy to the privacy of the solitary individual effectively sounds the death knell of the family as an organic unit with claims on its members.[2]

Since *Roe v Wade,* a succession of Supreme Court decisions on abortion has furthered the tendency to dissolve the family as an organic unit into a random collection of its current members. In *Planned Parenthood of Central Missouri v Danforth* (1976), Justice Blackmun, speaking for the majority, averred that the husband could not claim the right to terminate his wife's pregnancy "when the State itself lacks the right."[3] By the logic of *Danforth,* the husband has no more stake in his wife's pregnancy than any other individual, which effectively strips him of any stake in the family and strips the family of any standing as an organic unit. More disturbing, as Tiffany R. Jones and Larry Peterman argue, *Danforth,* by shredding the husband's stake in children, establishes that "there is nothing of one's own in the most serious sense left for husbands in the family."[4] In *Planned Parenthood of Southeastern Pennsylvania v Casey* (1992), the Court reinforced and extended the logic of *Danforth,* arguing that a husband "has no enforceable right to require a wife to advise him before she exercises her personal choices." Not merely does a wife have no obligation to obtain her husband's consent for an abortion, she has no obligation to notify him she is having one. In the Court's opinion, the notion of a husband's interest in his wife's pregnancy reflects "a different understanding of the family"[5] than that which prevails today.

In *Casey,* the majority of the Court explained the social and economic assumptions that informed its views: Women, the justices argued, had become accustomed to the free disposition of their sexuality and labor, and unplanned pregnancies should not be allowed to interfere with their ability to support themselves. The opinion amounted to a proclamation that the family has so decomposed that no woman or child could automatically count on its support, and an admission that no woman should expect the government to pick up the slack. If a woman can afford a child, she may decide to carry her pregnancy to term. If she cannot, she must have easy access to abortion. Feminists extend the defense of abortion as an individual right even to very young women on the grounds that a woman's sexuality is a purely individual matter. Such radical notions of individualism further undercut the view of children as a familial and social responsibility, effectively casting them as individual possessions to be disposed of at will. It should make us thoughtful that, on this point, the largest business interests and the feminist activists agree.

Critics and advocates of women's sexual liberation agree that the opening of opportunities for women and the sexual revolution have unfolded in tandem, but they differ about the consequences. Critics insist that women's rejection of their traditional responsibilities is resulting in the abolition of marriage, the destruction of the family, and the abandonment of children. Advocates counter that the freedom to leave a marriage or never marry at all is essential to a woman's well-being; that the traditional family, "the cradle of women's oppression," is being replaced by newer, healthier relations; and that children do better when their mother is happy and fulfilled. The passion of both groups admits little common ground and, especially, discourages a reasoned assessment of our situation.

The unfolding of the debate has made it difficult to deplore the consequences of the sexual revolution without appearing to condemn women. At the same time, it is difficult to defend the increased independence of women without also defending their sexual liberation. Yet the question remains: Does the increased independence of women require their sexual liberation? Or to put it differently, Does sexual liberation strengthen the independence of women? Secular feminists answer both questions with a resounding yes and insist that abortion constitutes the linchpin of both. These questions do not much trouble opponents of women's liberation, for they find little more to applaud in the growing personal independence of women than in their sexual liberation. Under these conditions, it is almost impossible to criticize the sexual liberation of women without appearing also to oppose their increased independence.

What the debate in this form obscures is the close relationship between the sexual liberation of women—appropriately known as the sexual revolution—and the disintegration of the family. Contrary to the popular assumption that "living together" helps prepare a couple for marriage, couples who cohabitate before marriage are less satisfied with their partnerships and less committed to their partners than married couples.[6] If they marry, they are also more likely to get divorced than those who did not cohabitate before marriage.[7] The problems with cohabitation underscore the perils of sexual liberation for the women it purportedly benefits. Feminists dismiss evocations of natural differences between women and men as evidence of repressive and stereotypical attitudes. In their view, patriarchal men have invented the alleged differences in order to perpetuate men's control of women. Yet recent scholarship confirms the age-old wisdom that young women and young men have different sexual agendas: Young men are much more eager for sexual relations with their steady girlfriends than are the girlfriends, who are primarily seeking emotional commitment.[8] The sexual liberation of women thus serves the interests of young men while compromising those of young women.

In practice, the sexual liberation of women has realized men's most predatory sexual fantasies. As women shook themselves free from the norms and conventions of sexual conduct, men did the same. Where once young men had been expected to respect a young woman's no, they might now plausibly assume that the no really means yes. They might err in the assumption, sometimes at the heavy cost of being accused of rape, but not because any social rules discouraged sex between unmarried young people. Where but recently a young woman's unintended pregnancy would have led to a shotgun wedding, it now leads to abortion or single motherhood. Indeed, George Akerlof, Janet Yellen, and Michael Katz have demonstrated that the increased availability of abortion and contraception in the late 1960s and early 1970s led directly to the dramatic rise in births to single mothers. They plausibly reason that ready access to contraception and abortion seriously undercuts young women's—and their fathers'—ability to use a possible pregnancy as a means to avoid sex before marriage or to secure a promise of marriage should a pregnancy occur. In this climate, increasing numbers of young women appear, however misguidedly, to have used sexual acquiescence rather than sexual abstinence to attract and hold a man. The skyrocketing number of out-of-wedlock births and the declining rate of marriage testify to their miscalculation. But the young women who tried to cling to traditional norms of propriety fared no better. With easy access to women who had no objections to premarital sex, men had no incentive to meet the demands of women who sought to trade sex for marriage.[9]

It is not surprising that young men who can obtain sex without marriage defer marriage or avoid it entirely. But men's preference for freedom over commitment comes at a price: George Akerlof argues that the decline in marriage among lower- and working-class men has led to the rise in crime, drug use, and underemployment and that these trends have a multiplier effect. As the percentage of unmarried men in a community rises, community acceptance of not marrying rises as well, with a concomitantly greater tolerance for the hooliganism of bands of under- or unemployed single men.[10] We need not minimize the toll that these patterns extract from the other members of the community, notably women and children, in order to recognize that the heaviest toll ultimately falls on the men themselves. Men like to think of themselves as dodging the "trap" of marriage, but marriage is, if anything, more necessary to their well-being than to that of women.

Marriage is also essential to the well-being of children, and children tend to increase the solidity of a marriage. But children are consciously and unconsciously discriminating: To them, marriage means their two biological parents. Children who grow up in a household with both of their biological parents are, on average, better off than children who grow up in a household with only one biological parent, regardless of the parent's race, educational background, or even whether that parent was married when the child was born or whether he or she remarries.[11] Boys who do not live with both of their biological parents are twice as likely as other boys to end up in prison; girls are seven times as likely to be abused by a stepfather as by a biological father; both boys and girls who grow up with a single parent are two or three times more likely to have emotional problems and twice as likely to get divorced as children from an intact nuclear family.[12] These miseries do not begin to exhaust the handicaps that burden the children of divorced or never married parents. Children do not thrive on divorce or single parenthood, yet more than half of the children born in 1994 will spend some or all of their childhood in a single-parent home, and as of 1992, approximately half of all first marriages were projected to end in divorce.

Does Equality Put a Marriage at Risk?

At the dawn of the third millennium, the institution of marriage—and, consequently, the child-friendly family life that depends on it—is at high risk. A scant half of adult Americans live in heterosexual marriages (54.4 percent); barely one-quarter of all households include a married couple and children; almost one-third of all American children are born to a single mother (the figure jumps to almost 70 percent among African Americans); and one-quarter of American children live in a family headed by a single mother. All of these figures represent substantial changes within roughly the last thirty-five years. During that period, women's fertility dropped dramatically, while out-of-wedlock births grew by 26 percent, and families headed by single mothers by 13 percent.[13] Nothing suggests that these patterns will automatically reverse themselves in the immediate future, and we may reasonably assume that without a renewed moral and cultural commitment, neither marriages nor two-parent families will fully regain their standing as foundational social institutions.[14]

Contrary to feminist hopes and expectations, traditional gender roles and values tend to promote the strength and stability of marriages. Thus, couples in which men share domestic tasks with their wives are more likely to divorce than those in which they do not; those in which the man earns more than 50 percent of the family's income are less likely to divorce than those in which he does not; and the larger the share of the family's income the wife earns, the more likely her husband is to abuse her.[15] Many feminists have a deep stake in the idea of egalitarian marriages, believing that women will never be equal to men until husbands and wives share all responsibilities and have virtually interchangeable roles. Polls suggest that many Americans agree that the ideal marriage is one in which both husband and wife contribute to the family's income and to domestic labor and child-rearing. And empirical studies confirm that many married couples are indeed sharing responsibilities, although not always equally.

The erosion of the family as a distinct corporate unit has encouraged people to view marriage as a contract like any other and has fed the feminist insistence that the parties to it must enjoy equal rights. Unfortunately, the insistence on equality of roles increases the pressure on the marriage and often decreases both partners' investment in it. The equality of roles reinforces the idea of marriage as a contract and serves to protect each partner's self-interest as a hedge against divorce. Neither women nor men are likely to make compromises, much less sacrifices, for the good of the family as a whole if they do not expect the marriage to survive. And women are especially reluctant to put a career temporarily on hold if they have reason to think that they—and their children—may have to depend on their salary. Yet if both husband and wife resist making a wholehearted commitment to the marriage, the odds that the marriage will fail increase. Mistrust feeds mistrust, and while both partners watch out for their individual interests, their marriage and their children suffer. The predictable divorce rate merely drives home the lesson that marriage and family life require a good deal more than the defense of one's individual rights. As Danielle Crittenden writes, the family "has never been about the promotion of rights but the surrender of them— by *both* the man and the woman."[16]

The emphasis on individual rights at the expense of mutual responsibility and service underscores the connection between the sexual liberation of women and the decisive weakening of families and worsening condition of many children. The point is emphatically not to blame women, many of whom have also suffered from these developments. The larger, and I believe, incontestable, point is that the release of sexual taboos and protections that encircled women has effectively unleashed those taboos on society as a whole and, hence, on the lives of children who are not prepared to deal with them. The sexual liberation of women, combined with the feminist campaign against marriage and motherhood as the special vocation of women, has directly contributed to the declining birthrate, the proliferation of single-parent or single-mother families, and the number of children born outside of marriage. As women increasingly move into positions of direct professional and economic competition with men, they increasingly postpone marriage and childbirth or forgo them entirely. The growing economic independence of women also permits those who choose to do so to bear and raise a child without the cooperation of the child's father. At the same time, the ethos of sexual liberation has destroyed the stigma that condemned women for sexual activity outside of marriage. Many welcome these trends as progress for women, who are finally shaking off the shackles that bound them to dependence on men and thwarted their development as individuals.

Conservative women, in contrast, often campaign vigorously for family values but too often show no inclination to pay for services that might help less affluent Americans hold their families together. For better or worse, we have moved well beyond the point at which it is realistic simply to exhort people to do the right thing. Even many Christians have embraced women's liberation as a fulfillment of their personal and spiritual potential, and the calls for equality between spouses ring as loudly in many Christian circles as secular ones. The Christian emphasis on sexual equality in the family as well as in worldly roles confirms the pervasive impact of the sexual and economic revolution of the late 1960s. In effect, many Christians have embraced the spirit—and frequently the specific demands—of the secular discourse of individual rights.

4

Parents and Children

Francis Fukuyama has dubbed the cataclysmic sexual and economic revolution a "great disruption," which it incontestably has been. Many of Fukuyama's claims and conclusions invite debate and critical scrutiny, but one aspect of his argument commands serious attention: The new economic forces and systems that have come to dominate global life systematically erode institutionalized family life.[1] To be blunt, the new multinational economic giants have no need for stable families, which may actually interfere with their ability to manage workers and sell goods. Under these conditions, we cannot expect the world of production to foster the restoration of a responsible and ordered social and moral life. In the event of a crisis, political or social forces might attempt to impose order from above. But only organized religion—in the broad ecumenical sense—has the resources to promote and nurture a lasting moral renewal. Thus far, the mainstream Christian churches have showed little enthusiasm for condemning the disintegrative forces out of hand.

Fukuyama claims that people will instinctively back away from social chaos and generate new moral systems, and he finds signs that we are already doing so. He may be unduly sanguine. The popularity of Dr. Laura Schlessinger, however heartening, does not prove that a moral revival is underway. (Certain kinds of moral deviants seem to enjoy being spanked.) Individuals may respond to Dr. Laura's precepts and injunctions without substantively rethinking their individualist premises, notably their commitment to their individual rights.

In the United States, the responsibility to embody moral precepts has always been disproportionately ascribed to women, who have been noticeably more likely than men to practice Christian virtue in everyday life. Today, however, feminism has taught us to view women's traditional responsibilities as a form of oppression, and as women "move beyond" or graduate from the practice of those virtues, we are left with fewer and fewer people who do practice them. We are not, I think, likely to bring society closer to the practice of Christian virtue by representing the practice of virtue as the punitive confinement or oppression of some by others (women by men) and by identifying individual happiness with liberation from that alleged oppression.

Liberation from Morals?

Implicitly and explicitly, feminists have fostered the belief that the liberation of women must begin with their release from enforced servitude to children as well as to men. We have moved far from the sentimental pieties that enjoined women to find their greatest self-fulfillment in motherhood—the bearing and rearing of children. Popular psychology has led us from the painful recognition that mothers who lived vicariously through their children were likely to thwart the children's development to the self-congratulatory wisdom that children flourish precisely when their mother lives for herself rather than them. No working mother willingly assumes the guilt that she is sacrificing her children's well-being for her own, and fewer and fewer people are willing to tell working mothers that they are harming their children. Most of us acknowledge that many women must work if their families are to make ends meet, and in many specific instances the children, understanding this necessity, also understand that their well-being does rank as their mother's primary concern.

The problem does not so much lie in individual cases, which vary dramatically, as in society and our culture as a whole, for the social, economic, and sexual liberation of women have flooded the dikes of prudence, propriety, and self-restraint that protected children from the most dangerous adult transgressions. Today, it has become common to condemn the hypocritical fiction that divided the world into public and private spheres, primarily because women's ascription to the private sphere served to bar them from the freedoms enjoyed by men. But this argument fails to acknowledge that the mores—fiction, if you prefer—that sheltered women sheltered children as well. From the moment that public displays of sexuality and violence are accepted as inherent aspects of human nature, not to mention as individual rights to freedom of expression, they begin to penetrate the daily consciousness and experience of children.

Perhaps worse, the acceptance of public displays of sexuality and violence as individual rights effectively destroys the ideal of binding moral norms. By definition, when morality becomes a matter of personal preference, it ceases to be a binding social norm, and personal preference is merely the logical application of the consumer choice vigorously promoted by global corporations. The discrediting of binding social norms in turn undermines our ability to protect children, who themselves are now seen to enjoy virtually the same individual rights as adults. Thus do we fashion a world in which nine-, ten-, and eleven-year-old girls can reprove parents who attempt to censure their dress or behavior, defiantly insisting, "It is my life, and I can choose how to live it." Indeed, we have reached the point at which a television ad features a whining brat who badgers his mother into buying him a toy while the mature voice-over intones, "Children get what they want, why shouldn't you?"

In welcoming women into the ranks of masterless individuals, our society has decisively privileged individual choices, dubbed "individual rights," over any conception of the common good.[2] With breathtaking cynicism, it has paraphrased the insidious corporate slogan "What's good for General Motors is good for the country" and announced that the common good consists of the sum of individual choices. The measure of our denial of the limits imposed by a common existence lies in our reluctance to acknowledge that choice inevitably and necessarily refers to what one forgoes as well as what one gains. Jesus left no doubt on this point:

> For where your treasure is, there will your heart be also. . . . If therefore the light that is in thee be darkness, how great is that darkness! No man can serve two masters: for either he will hate the one, and love the other; or else he will hold to the one, and despise the other. Ye cannot serve God and mammon.
>
> Matthew 6:21, 23–24

Well may we protest that it is not "fair" that women bear the burden of protecting some conception of collective ideals whether of prudence or of charity, but fairness in the sense of equal opportunity to sin is hardly the point.

Traditionally, Christianity has fostered a more nuanced view of the claims of individuals. From the start, Christianity emphasized the direct relationship between each individual and God, both his love for the particular individual and the individual's personal accountability to him. Indeed, the Christian vision of moral responsibility has always depended on an acknowledgment of the responsibility of each individual, who is held to love God and neighbor and who is judged for each failure to observe God's commandments.

In this respect, Christianity introduced the very notion of the freedom and equality of individuals into world history.[3] In this equality before God's judgment and within his love lies the meaning of Paul's letter to the Galatians: "For ye are all the children of God by faith in Christ Jesus. For as many of you as have been baptized into Christ have put on Christ. There is neither Jew nor Greek, there is neither bond nor free, there is neither male nor female: for ye are all one in Christ Jesus" (3:26–28).

Modern admirers of this passage too often forget that Paul did not intend to transform the standing of and relations among people in the world. Neither the Gospels nor the other books of the New Testament condemn slavery. Nor do they promote worldly equality between women and men. Paul cautions his listeners against abusing the liberty that they enjoy as Christians:

> For, brethren, ye have been called unto liberty; only use not liberty for an occasion to the flesh, but by love serve one another. . . . But if ye bite and devour one another, take heed that ye be not consumed one of another. . . . If we live in the Spirit, let us also walk in the Spirit. Let us not be desirous of vain glory, provoking one another, envying one another.
>
> Galatians 5:13, 15, 25–26

Firmly condemning "adultery, fornication, uncleanness, lasciviousness, idolatry, witchcraft, hatred, variance, emulations, wrath, strife, seditions, heresies, envyings, murders, drunkenness, revellings, and such like," Paul reminds the Galatians that they are called to "love, joy, peace, longsuffering, gentleness, goodness, faith, meekness, temperance" (Gal. 5:19–21, 22–23).

Fervent advocates of women's rights like to read texts of this kind as admonitions against men's ideas of their superior status, but Paul's words are more plausibly read as a warning to women and men, both of whom are called on to live their specific (allotted) role in true Christian spirit.

Christian feminists frequently complain that men appear not to have taken Paul's injunctions much to heart. From the observation that men have felt free to ignore those claims it is a short step to the view that the principles of fairness and equality should relieve women of their observance as well. What proponents of this logic fail to acknowledge is that this liberation of women all but guarantees the triumph of people's "devouring" and being "consumed one of another." Others argue that men and women must equally work to restore the stability and vitality of families, and the argument is superficially seductive. In practice, many fathers are assuming a growing responsibility for the household and the rearing of children, and the trend is heartening. But the argument for equality is deeply flawed. In the first instance, we have the disquieting spectacle of the woman who effectively says to her husband, "I won't devote myself to children, husband, and family unless you do every bit as much as I do." Altogether more important, the argument for equality rests on the very individualist principles that are dismembering the family as a unit. In the end, if one takes the needs of children and the imitation of Christ seriously, "I want equal time off" does not cut it.

Christian Freedom

No person of faith or goodwill can doubt that women have too often carried excessively heavy domestic burdens and received too little respect in return. Today, many Christian churches are trying to rectify what they now see as their mistakes. Unfortunately, they are tending to take their models of justice to women from the secular world, thereby espousing premises that fundamentally contradict the tenets of their own faith. Consider the words of Mary Stewart Van Leeuwen, who informs "religiously committed people" that if they wish to defend the two-parent family, they should focus less on claiming the moral high ground and more on demonstrating through example their commitment "to egalitarian gender relations between spouses, to a radical degendering of both public and private spheres of life, and to the development of institutions supportive of childrearing that promote both female achievement and male nurturance."[4] Van Leeuwen, to her dismay, finds religious leaders sorely lacking in this regard. Yet she has taken her language and premises directly from secular feminism, which invites us to wonder whether she believes Christianity has anything to contribute to the discussion—or even whether the two-parent family has an intrinsic value.

Toward the close of Gail Godwin's novel, *The Good Husband,* Father Birkenshaw, a dying abbot, tells his protégé, Francis Lake, "You know, Francis, just as the monks kept learning alive in the Dark Ages, it's going to be people like you who keep human kindness and charity alive in ours."[5] Francis, who had left the novitiate to marry the flamboyant English professor Magda Danvers, is the good husband of Godwin's title, and his virtues are those attributed by the Book of Proverbs (31:10–31) to the good wife: human kindness, industry, and charity—the virtues of service and sacrifice. Today, women are wresting themselves from the bonds of those virtues, and, as they do, the virtues are all but disappearing. Many—and not only women—do still practice service and sacrifice, but the injunctions to do so have all but evaporated. Increasingly, our culture at large is quick to see injunctions of all kinds, especially those previously directed at women, as signs of servitude, specifically, of women's imposed subservience to men. In this climate, few women or men are inclined to risk instructing women in their "duty" to others for fear of inviting charges of sexism. Godwin's genius lies in attributing those virtues to a man, thereby challenging us to see their grace and power without reference to sex.

The pervasive sense that women were punitively held accountable for the practice of the virtues of service and sacrifice has, more often than not, resulted in the conviction that justice entitles women to freedom from that practice. Women's freedom in this regard—whatever its positive contributions to women's dignity and self-respect—has led to a discrediting of the virtues. The logic seems to be that if feminists are correct in viewing women's "traditional" work as nothing more than servants' work, then only servants should be expected to do it. (Although how women then justify imposing it on men may deserve attention.) The demands and undeniable sacrifice imposed by those virtues tempt us to lose sight of their intrinsic value and to agree with the secular feminist verdict that they represent markers of women's oppression. Convinced by the spurious logic that women who lived under the domination of men were coerced into the practice of self-abnegating virtue, many insist that the liberation of women must begin with their liberation from service to and sacrifice for others. Lost in this reasoning is the recognition of the centrality of virtues to the meaning of human life.

This challenge, however, is not one we are likely to meet if we continue to focus on the rights and liberation of the individual as an intrinsic good. Christians, especially, have always understood that the greater freedom is not the freedom *from* but the freedom *for.* As the chickens of our liberationist and individualistic priorities come home to roost, many women, especially, let us hope, Christian women, are beginning to understand that the price of radical individualism is too high. But many continue to choke on the notion that they might be called to somewhat different roles and somewhat different sacrifices than men. In our time, those differences are smaller than ever in our history, but the very similarity of much of men's and women's experience in so many areas of life apparently makes the abiding differences more difficult than ever to accept.

The greatest danger of all may lie in the dissemination of sexual egalitarianism within our churches, for the core of Christianity has always lain in the simultaneous reality of our particularity and our universality. God does not love mankind; he loves each man, woman, and child, precisely for his or her particular being in a particular body. And he loves each of us equally because he is capable of loving each of us in particular. Our democracy insists on the separation of church and state, but that separation has never foreclosed a deep Christian influence on our political institutions and traditions. Now, as so often in the past, it has become necessary to renew that influence—to bring a Christian understanding of sexual difference and human equality to redress the excesses of the ideology of individual rights. And there would be no better place to begin than with the complementarity of women and men and their joint stewardship for children. Otherwise, we are in danger of mistaking the red and lowering morning sky for the red sky of a promising evening.

Post-feminism and a New Gender Covenant

Response by Stanley J. Grenz

After the heyday of activism, which tended to require that every would-be combatant enter the fray as either a strident feminist or a no-nonsense traditionalist, we seem to be tip-toeing into a day in which the two positions no longer appear as the only alternatives. Today, several voices are suggesting what would have seemed impossible only a few years ago, namely, that one can value the advances that have been made in the name of women, while acknowledging that the gain has not come without a corresponding loss and that whatever victories have been won have also extracted a great

Stanley J. Grenz is professor of theology and ethics at Carey Theological College and Regent College, both in Vancouver, and at Northern Baptist Theological Seminary in Lombard, Illinois. An ordained Baptist minister, he earned his Ph.D. at the University of Munich in Germany. Among his many books are *The Moral Quest: Foundations of Christian Ethics* (InterVarsity Press, 1997); *Women in the Church: A Biblical Theology of Women in Ministry* (InterVarsity Press, 1995); and *Created for Community: Connecting Christian Belief with Christian Living* (Baker, 1998).

toll, especially on the family as an institution and more particularly on the nation's children. In short, today it is possible to be both a feminist (if by this designation one means a person who believes that women and men ought to be acknowledged as having equal importance in society) and a traditionalist (that is, a person who accentuates the importance of the non-dissolvable distinctiveness of male and female). In her essay, Elizabeth Fox-Genovese indicates that she ought to be numbered among this group of "post-feminist traditionalists" or "post-traditionalist feminists."

In the following paragraphs, I indicate what I think are Professor Fox-Genovese's two major contributions in her essay, while elaborating on what for me are the seminal thoughts she presents. Then, after taking exception with her at a couple of places, I offer the point of my greatest disagreement, which opens up, I hope, an area of potential further conversation.

The Critique of Radical Individualism

In her helpful essay, Fox-Genovese offers an articulate example of the new mediating position vis-à-vis the feminist movement. Without slipping into a reactionary mode that calls for a return to some golden age in the past when women knew their place and were content to stay in it, Fox-Genovese nevertheless decries what she rightly sees as the misguided premise to which much feminist activism has appealed, namely, a radical individualist posture that threatens to undermine the institutions of marriage and the family so necessary for the well-being of our children. In so doing, she has identified a wider problem plaguing Western society in general. In many areas of contemporary life and in many of the social issues we face, we are seeing the unwholesome fruit of an unbridled individualism.

In decrying the radical individualism that motivates much of feminism, Fox-Genovese has put her finger on what we might label "the great mistake" lying at the heart of modern American life, if not of the entire Enlightenment heritage. We appear to be engaged in the misguided and ultimately doomed attempt to build a society on the unstable foundation of radical individualism with its attendant appeal to the rights of the individual.

Now let me state loudly and clearly that I believe—as I think Fox-Genovese does—that human rights are crucial to the well-being of society. Which of us would trade in our citizenship in this land with its great tradition of individual freedom and of championing the cause of the oppressed for that of any of the totalitarian regimes that litter the past and present world landscape? We must cherish the freedoms we enjoy in our land, and we must never give up speaking in support of and defending human rights wherever and whenever they are threatened.

At the same time, the assumptions that lie at the heart of the kind of radical individualism that seems rampant in the land—namely, that self-actualization is the highest (if not the sole) purpose for existence and that society is nothing more than a collection of individuals each pursuing his or her own private happiness—constitute too flimsy a foundation on which to build a viable and vibrant social order. In fact, the attempt to do so is based on what we might rightly call a theological heresy, namely, the belief that to be human means to be an isolated, self-enclosed individual. This heresy pictures human social life somewhat like a game of billiards, each ball existing as a complete unit in isolation from the others and the interaction between them being the result of one unit forcefully colliding with another. In contrast to radical individualism, biblical Christianity declares that to be human means to be persons-in-relationships, as many contemporary sociologists and psychologists have also come to realize.

Peter Berger and others have pointed out that the well-being of society requires that the social order be built on a transcendent vision that mediates to its members a sense that they are participants in something greater than what the day in and day out routines of their personal lives might suggest. This sense of participation in something transcendent, in turn, provides the basis for the construction of a meaningful personal identity. It is in this context that human rights become important, for human rights then uphold the importance of the identity of each participant in society. In addition to mediating rights to each citizen, however, the sense of our participating in something transcendent places on all members of society a responsibility to the other and a responsibility to the whole. This acceptance of responsibility, in turn, provides the proper context in which individual freedom together with the right to self-determination and self-actualization can exercise their rightful function. When advanced apart from this framework, the focus on the individual and on individual freedom all too readily leads to the destructive misuse of individual rights so evident in contemporary North American society.

Fox-Genovese reminds us of one lucid example of this. She points out the toll that the elevation of unbalanced freedom has taken on the family. And she rightly puts her finger on the sexual revolution—a topic that has been of special interest to me as well[1]—as being one crucial area in which unbridled freedom has had catastrophic consequences.

The Appeal to Self-Sacrifice

The second contribution I see in this lecture arises from Fox-Genovese's call for a balance between individual rights and a new virtue ethic. More particularly, she calls on women to cultivate once again the currently unpopular virtue of sacrifice, especially self-sacrifice for the sake of their children. At the foundation of her appeal is a great principle that has been a part of the Western tradition since the first century of our era but has been endangered by the activism of the last forty years, namely, the principle of personal sacrifice for the sake of others.

Although articulated by many people in many places, nowhere do we find this principle more poignantly displayed than in Jesus of Nazareth. In fact, the call to self-sacrifice and humble servanthood for the sake of the well-being of others is *the* central teaching of Jesus:

> You know that those who are regarded as rulers of the Gentiles lord it over them, and their high officials exercise authority over them. Not so with you. Instead, whoever wants to become great among you must be your servant, and whoever wants to be first must be slave of all.
>
> Mark 10:42–44 NIV

For Jesus these were not merely words of advice applicable to others. Rather, what he taught, he also lived out. According to Mark's account, Jesus then added, "For even the Son of Man did not come to be served, but to serve, and to give his life as a ransom for many" (v. 45 NIV). For this reason, the New Testament writers proclaim Jesus as the great paradigm of God's desire for human living:

> Your attitude should be the same as that of Christ Jesus: Who, being in very nature God, did not consider equality with God something to be grasped, but made himself nothing, taking the very nature of a servant, being made in human likeness. And being found in appearance as a man, he humbled himself and became obedient to death—even death on a cross!
>
> Philippians 2:5–8 NIV

The call for self-sacrifice after the pattern of Jesus lies at the heart of the New Testament ethic. As a result, the biblical writers repeatedly and consistently call on the "strong" voluntarily to set aside their privilege for the sake of the "weak."

By pointing out that the feminist focus on the right of women to self-actualization has undercut the "nurturing stewardship of families and children," Fox-Genovese has drawn our attention back to this biblical ethic in a day in which it is being marginalized both by the attack of its foes and the neglect of its traditional advocates. But Jesus' teaching, coming as it does from a male, makes it clear that this ethic is for all, not just for women, in contrast to what seems to be the tone of Fox-Genovese's essay. More importantly, in applying the principle that the strong should sacrifice for the sake of the weak within the context of the family, the New Testament clearly indicates that husbands rather than wives—and hence that men more so than women—are to take the lead in living out the virtue of self-sacrifice (e.g., Eph. 5:25).

Post-feminism and Gender Roles

I could spend the remainder of my response taking issue with Fox-Genovese over some of the minor details of her essay. For example, I wonder what exactly constitutes the family that feminism has undermined and whether the nuclear family is as normative or sacrosanct as she seems to imply, especially when we view human social interaction from a longer, historical perspective. Further, from her passing remarks about these matters, I sense that I differ with Fox-Genovese on such matters as the nature and value of separation of church and state and the significance of the declining birthrate.

I could likewise spend some time voicing my disagreements about some of the major issues she raises. For example, contrary to Fox-Genovese, I think that the feminist revolution, despite the negative results some of its excesses have produced, has been generally positive. More significantly, I come away from her essay uneasy about the shape of her positive proposal, which, as I read it, is that within marriage men and especially women ought to assume once again their traditional gender roles. Hence, on the basis of recent divorce and abuse statistics, Fox-Genovese claims that "traditional gender roles and values tend to promote the strength and stability of marriages."

While I am sympathetic to what she is seeking to accomplish, at this point I fear I must part company with her. Fox-Genovese's appeal to divorce and abuse tendencies entails a grossly oversimplified reading of a complex phenomenon. Traditional marriages may be less prone to divorce. In many cases, however, this may have less to do with any sense that spouses may have that they are fulfilling the roles for which they were created than that women in such situations perceive themselves as having no alternative but to remain in an unfulfilling relationship.

But my uneasiness lies at an even more fundamental level. I too acknowledge the basic difference between males and females. But what is more difficult to determine is what that difference entails and how such differences ought to find expression in the roles that women and men fulfill in their various relationships, including within marriage. And things get even more complicated when we suggest that a particular model of relationships is normative for all married couples. It is precisely here that Fox-Genovese is most imprecise, and this imprecision causes me concern. I want to know what exactly she sees as the fundamental differences between females and males, what exactly she concludes are their implications for female-male relationships, and whether she views her conclusions as normative for all.

I find that those who accentuate role distinctions today often propound the idea that men are created to lead and women to follow. Note this typical definition: "At the heart of mature masculinity is a sense of benevolent responsibility to lead, provide for and protect women in ways appropriate to a man's differing relationships," and in the same way, "at the heart of mature femininity is a freeing disposition to affirm, receive and nurture strength and leadership

from worthy men in ways appropriate to a woman's differing relationships."[2] This understanding of the essence of
manhood and womanhood quite readily translates into defined roles in human relationships that are elevated to normative status. Man is to lead, woman to support; man is to
initiate, woman to enable; man is to take responsibility for
the well-being of woman, woman to take responsibility for
helping man.[3]

The widespread acceptance of this characterization
might lead to the kind of stable marriages for which Professor Fox-Genovese is with good reason an eloquent propo-
nent. But this definition simply does not fit all women and
men very well, nor, in fact, any particular woman or man.
Leadership, provision, and protection do not flow between
the sexes in a one-way manner but rather bidirectionally.

I am not suggesting that Fox-Genovese holds to this particular definition of masculinity and femininity. Nevertheless, many today see the male-as-leader female-as-fol-
lower model as synonymous with the traditional view and
as the only valid alternative to the egalitarian marriages
that Fox-Genovese herself critiques. Rather than an affirmation of inflexible gender roles, however, I believe that
the current situation calls for more flexible understandings
of role differentiations, understandings that encourage
couples to find the kind of mutuality that best suits them
and their relationship.[4]

A New Male-Female Covenant

This leads me to the central point at which I must re-
spectfully demur with Fox-Genovese. In contrast to her
stated conviction, I am convinced that Paul's great "charter
of freedom"—to cite Paul Jewett's descriptor—"There is neither Jew nor Greek, slave nor free, male nor female, for you
are all one in Christ Jesus" (Gal. 3:28 NIV), does indeed have
"necessary implications for relations in this world." More

importantly, I think *Paul* was convinced of this, again contrary to Fox-Genovese's stated position. I think the apostle believed that our fundamental unity in Christ has far-reaching implications for human social interaction in the church, if not in the wider society as well. This text requires not only that we take seriously the implications of the soteriological relativizing of ethnic distinctions ("neither Jew nor Greek") and of socioeconomic realities ("neither slave nor free"), but also that we seek to understand what the unity of "male and female" in Christ means for human relations.

From my perspective, the greatest challenge we face this side of the feminist-traditionalist culture war is the task of entering as women and men into a new covenant that can lead us into godly male-female relationships. Such relationships, I believe, would protect the fundamental equality of each person—both male and female—while acknowledging the differences that mark us as either female or male. Although I do not have the space to go into great detail, let me suggest that three profoundly theological considerations—that is, beliefs grounded in the Christian conception of God—point us in this direction.

First, this new covenant finds its foundation in the pattern of relationality that characterizes the Triune God as disclosed in the life of Jesus. More specifically, in their quest for godly relationships, men and women ought to take seriously the fundamental mutuality exhibited between Jesus the Son and his heavenly Father.

Second, this new covenant looks for its goal in our common human task as purposed by God. This means that in their pursuit of godly relationships, women and men should direct their life together toward the common human calling to reflect the divine character and thereby the image of God. Rather than being the *imago dei* in isolation from each other, however, it is in our relationality that we image God. More specifically, God's character comes into view as through the Holy Spirit we love one another, whether as partners who share the exclusive love relationship of marriage or as participants in the more inclusive nonmarital bonds that bring persons—both male and female—together, especially within the context of Christ's fellowship.

Within this fellowship, our task is to help others, in the words of Jean Vanier, founder of the worldwide l'Arche communities, to "grow toward wholeness and to discover [our] place, and eventually exercise [our] gifts, in a network of friendship."[5] This observation leads to the third aspect. The new covenant between women and men discovers the means to its goal in the divine way of life revealed in Jesus. In his life and above all in his death, Jesus indicated that the mutuality and love he shared with the one he called Father through the divine Holy Spirit entailed an eternal empowerment by each of the other, an empowerment that binds the three trinitarian persons together as the one God. In our quest for godly relationships, in turn, as women and men we must likewise realize that we exist for the other—that even whatever distinctions may characterize us as female and male serve to enhance the other—with the result that we seek to discover expressions of our fundamental interdependence that empower both.[6]

As these remarks suggest, while not intending to ignore the public sphere nor the issues connected to the social institutions in our nation, in the end my chief concern is for the community that gathers around the name of Jesus. I desire that the church look to its Lord and thereby provide a much needed, positive alternative in the midst of the culture war sparked by the feminist movement and its traditionalist backlash. My concern lies here because I am convinced that if the nation is to be renewed, then renewal must begin with the church. "For it is time for judgment to begin with the family of God" (1 Peter 4:17 NIV). Yet unfortunately the church has often been, and sometimes continues to be, the place of injustice not justice, especially toward women.

It was spring semester 1997. A woman in my theology course came to me after a class in which I had been lecturing on ecclesiology. "I perceive you to be a person who loves the body of Christ," she said to me. "I want to make an appointment to see you," she added, "because I find myself losing my love for Christ's body." In my office she later divulged the root of her difficulty. "I fear that there is no place for me to minister with my gifts in the church," she confessed. "There is no place for me because I am a woman." What followed was a sad but poignant verbal sketch of her deepest feelings climaxed by words I will never forget. "This is my image of the church," she explained. "Across the room stands Jesus. He is looking this way. Encircling the Lord and gazing on his face is a group of men standing shoulder to shoulder. Standing on the outside, I wonder, *Can I somehow elbow my way into that circle?*"

The time has come for us to close the chapter on attitudes and situations that result in the sense of exclusion this woman felt. As Christians, our goal ought to be to seek the Spirit's wisdom so that by the Spirit's power we might be a people who pioneer a relationality between women and men that is wholesome and godly, and as such advances God's purposes, namely, to bring about the fullness of the new community God intends for all creation. And becoming this kind of people in the contemporary post-feminist context requires that before God we seal a new gender covenant, a covenant that focuses on the kind of mutuality between women and men that is life-giving, empowering, and edifying of each woman and man, and that fosters wholesome nurturing within marriages, within family structures, within church fellowships, and in turn, within society as a whole.

Sexual Difference
and Human Equality

Response by Mardi Keyes

Professor Elizabeth Fox-Genovese argues persuasively that modern American individualism stands at the heart of the breakdown of the family. And while radical individualism motivates both men and women, she suggests that the recent undermining of family and children can in some important ways be traced to individualistic feminism and its obsession with equal rights. In other words, feminist "progress" for women may have come at "an exorbitantly high price"—the price of stable families and the welfare of children.

Margaret (Mardi) Drew Keyes has been since 1979 co-director, with her husband, of L'Abri Fellowship, a residential study center, in Southborough, Massachusetts. A graduate of Wellesley College, she has worked with L'Abri centers in Switzerland and England. A frequent speaker on Christianity and feminism, Ms. Keyes has also published on feminism and the Bible, children and their work, the problem of evil, and homosexuality.

Fox-Genovese ends her lecture with a warning and challenge directed specifically to Christians. She sees the repudiation of different roles and responsibilities within the family as a capitulation to secular feminist individualism and a major contributor to the collapse of family life. She challenges Christians to renew "a deep Christian influence on our political institutions and traditions" by bringing "a Christian understanding of sexual difference and human equality to redress the excesses of the ideology of individual rights. And there would be no better place to begin than with the complementarity of women and men and their joint stewardship for children."

In my response to Fox-Genovese, I would like to pick up this important challenge. It is not a simple one, because "a Christian understanding" of the sexes is by no means self-evident. While some parts of the church today *have* been co-opted by a thoroughly secular, individualistic egalitarianism, other parts, in the name of "complementarity," are equally captive to a rigid traditionalism that stigmatizes women who work outside the home, even for financial necessity, and discourages fathers from hands-on intimate care of their children. Christian history cannot be our authority, as it is full of a mixture of good and bad gender ideas and practices. Women have been barred from higher education and the professions, forbidden to speak in public, denied the vote, forced to publish under male names, and even beaten by their husbands, all in the name of the Christian God and female virtue, and in service of gender "complementarity."

So how do we determine the "Christian understanding of sexual difference and human equality"? I will try to consider some of the relevant biblical teaching on gender and to distinguish absolute norms from areas of freedom. I believe this is the only way for Christians to avoid our culture's polarization and the danger of thinking and living out of reaction to either feminist or traditionalist extremes.

While I am in 100-percent sympathy with Fox-Genovese's passionate concern for strong and stable families and the needs of children, I find some of her analysis of the causes of family breakdown confusing. Her discussion of the relationship of sexual freedom, legal abortion, and the slow dissolution of the family as an organic unit, and the costly implications of that loss, is extremely insightful and clear. What I find problematic is the assumed connection between marital equality (defined as shared roles, responsibilities, and virtues) on the one hand, and on the other, a contractual, uncommitted model of marriage in which individual rights are paramount and neither spouse is willing to "make compromises, much less sacrifices, for the good of the family as a whole."

This connection between equality and contractual marriage is sometimes stated and often implied by innuendo in a way that suggests there is a necessary and even causal relationship between the two. Within a secular, individualistic worldview, these ideas *are* often found together, and they surely do increase the odds of marital failure. But within the biblical understanding of covenant marriage, marital equality—including shared roles, responsibilities, and virtues—is thoroughly consistent with a "wholehearted commitment to marriage." Biblical marriage is a lifelong covenant, not a tentative contract. Within it, husbands and wives are both called to service and self-sacrifice, and there is room for enormous flexibility of roles, without in any way denying the created sex difference. Christian marriage is a "third way," which avoids the common inflexibility and dogmatism of both traditionalism and individualistic feminism. These ideas will become clearer as I look at the relevant biblical teaching.

Situating Ourselves within the Biblical Drama

When Christians think about the issues surrounding human equality and sexual difference, it is crucial for us to remember where we are historically and theologically within the biblical metanarrative. We are living in a world that was created "very good" but has been terribly marred by human rebellion against the Creator. Genesis 3 points explicitly to a gendered dimension to the fall. We know that male-female relations are no longer "very good" but a mixed bag, including good creational realities and fallen dispositions and behavioral patterns. But God, in his mercy, has intervened to redeem his broken, messy world. We live "between the times." We can know the firstfruits of redemption in gender relations, as in all areas of life. And we can look forward with certain hope to Christ's final redemption, when all things will be made right.

If we lived in a pre-fall world, there would be no competition between gender equality and justice and the needs of children and families. In a fallen world, there often is. But as we aim to live out the firstfruits of redemption, we find ourselves embracing all of these responsibilities and resisting the pressure of being polarized by them. The same Bible that establishes the equal dignity of men and women as image bearers of God and commands husbands to honor their wives as equal heirs of the gift of life also commands parents to nurture their children and warns of judgment on any who cause little children to stumble. The good of individuals is inseparable from the good of institutions, as is clear in the biblical metaphors of marriage as a mysterious union of head and body, and the church as one body with many members. Caring for the vulnerable, and for children in particular, inevitably means individual sacrifices, which in a biblical framework are meant to be shared by men and women.

For Christians, these are kingdom ideals to be aimed at, but with the recognition that in a fallen world we will not attain them perfectly. The Christian's allegiance is not to the ideology of equal rights, which Fox-Genovese critiques so well. Following Jesus, who willingly laid aside his equality with God to save us (Phil. 2:5–8), is inconsistent with an attitude that demands that each spouse does exactly the same amount of economic work, diaper changing, dishwashing, carpooling, and so on. In covenant marriage, both men and women must be willing to make unequal sacrifices when the well-being of children, each other, and the family are at stake. But what should women do if men don't do their part? That is one of Fox-Genovese's legitimate worries. Within a secular ideology of equal rights, women may well repudiate the virtues of service and self-sacrifice, with the attitude, "I won't devote myself to children, husband, and family unless you do every bit as much as I do." But for Christians, that attitude is not an option. Women must do the same thing that virtuous men do in a similar situation—pick up the slack, walk the extra mile, put their desires on the back burner, and serve those who need them.

I'd like to look now at some of the relevant biblical teaching about sexual difference and human equality as it relates to the family.

Human Equality and Sexual Difference

The biblical narrative begins with the clear affirmation that man and woman were created as equals, "in the image of God." We are equal in being and value. These ideas inspired the Declaration of Independence as well as the nineteenth-century liberal feminist crusade for the inclusion of women with all the men who had been created equal. These ideas also inspired the abolitionist movement for the inclusion of African Americans. Most of us in the West still take for granted the belief in human equality before God and understand equality before the law as a logical extension of that truth.

But the Bible's teaching on male and female equality does not imply exact sameness. When Adam was alone, God completed humanity and satisfied his need for "one of his kind" by the creation of a woman, not another man. There is a good God-given complementarity and interdependence to the sexes that affects us holistically but is most obvious in our procreational differences. True "women's liberation" is not dependent on overcoming pregnancy and lactation as some feminists have insisted.[1]

But what is the significance of our sexual complementarity? While the Bible is clear that the sex-gender difference is real and good and that men and women need each other, it is strikingly silent when it comes to defining our differences or their implications. For example, it never spells out any absolute, transcultural, psychological, cognitive, or emotional differences between men and women. It never defines "masculinity" or "femininity" and never exhorts men to be "manly" or women to be "womanly." So while androgyny is not a biblical goal, neither is a wooden conformity to any particular culture's gender definitions and prescriptions. The silence of the Bible implies mystery—think of Paul's description of marriage as a mysterious oneness of husband and wife (Eph. 5:32)—and encourages freedom for different individuals and cultures to express their sex-gender identity in a variety of ways. In fact, the main emphasis of the biblical writers is on the essential unity of the human race and our call to the same character goals and virtues. Men and women are to embody the beatitudes, to imitate Christ (not in his maleness but in his unfallen humanity), and to put on the armor of God (Eph. 6:11–17). Both sexes are to bear the same fruit of the Spirit, which is "love, joy, peace, patience, kindness, goodness, faithfulness, gentleness and self-control" (Gal. 5:22–23 NIV). The implication seems to be that if we aim for the virtues and imitate Christ, our gender identity will take care of itself. We will become the individual men and women God created us to be.

Similarly, the Bible does not prescribe absolute separate spheres and work roles on the basis of the sex difference. At creation, God addressed the first man and woman together with the shared responsibility to fill the earth and exercise dominion and care over it. He did not say, "Eve, be fruitful, change diapers, cook dinner, and clean the house—that's your role"; and "Adam, build culture—go into politics, business, academia, medicine, law, the arts, and the professions." The man and the woman were called then, and are still called, to the whole complex, multifaceted task of culture-building under God, including the producing and sustaining of families and work in the wider world. This joint call does not imply the exact sameness of man and woman. Our complementary male and female contributions are needed in all areas of life—public and private—to fulfill God's call to human stewardship over his creation.

Mary Stewart Van Leeuwen points out that every culture creates ways of expressing the sex-gender difference, including gendered divisions of labor, dress, rituals, manners, and dance, as a kind of sacramental testimony to our God-given, gender-role complementarity and interdependence. But the particular expressions and divisions of labor vary from culture to culture and throughout history. As Van Leeuwen puts it, "What is considered 'proper' for men or women to do varies greatly. But we have yet to find a culture in which there are no gender roles beyond the minimum needed for reproduction."[2] Ever since the fall, however, gender roles have not always been sensible or just. For example, in some cultures, women do the heavy labor and eat much less protein than the men, clearly neither a sensible nor just arrangement. In modern America, women with paid jobs tend to work a "second shift" at home, while men enjoy more leisure time. In a fallen world, gender roles can be distorted by legalism and become rigid cages. When this happens, Van Leeuwen writes, "then they cease to enhance and instead begin to stifle the God-given personhood of both women and men."[3]

Fox-Genovese's critique is directed at the feminist "heresy" of androgyny—those who minimize the sex difference. But radical feminism is guilty of the opposite, and in some ways, more serious heresy—of maximizing it. Men and women are two entirely different kinds of beings. So-called "women's ways" are glorified and "men's ways" are demonized. Ultimately, men are evil oppressors and women are innocent victims. Our essential equality as image bearers of God, who are equally fallen and by God's grace equally redeemable, is altogether lost. Our unity and interdependence are denied. Lesbian feminist separatists would love to dispense with men altogether but are still dependent on male sperm to exercise their "right" to be mothers.

To be faithful to both the admonitions and silences of the Bible, it appears we must walk a tightrope. We must not deny or repudiate the good created sex difference, but neither should we make more of it than the Bible does.

Sexual Difference, Human Equality, and Work

In applying these ideas to work, it matters that most men are physically stronger than most women and that pregnant and nursing women have an obvious gender specific vulnerability. Throughout history, the physical differences between men and women have frequently been used to justify unfair restrictions on women's lives, mobility, and work. But when feminists have denied these clear, commonsense differences in order to protect women's "equality," the denial has tended to backfire against women, particularly poorer women. It is no accident that working-class factory women resisted the Equal Rights Amendment, fearing that "gender equality" would mean "gender identity" and would strip them of hard-won protective legislation, exempting pregnant and nursing women from mandatory overtime and lifting heavy weights.

On the other hand, not all men are physically stronger than all women, and in some cultures and economies physical strength makes more difference than in others. It takes more strength to chop down trees or plow a field than to operate a computer. Furthermore, the special vulnerability associated with childbearing and nursing does not affect all women, and most mothers in the West today are affected by these vulnerabilities for a relatively short chapter of their working lives. Christians who prescribe absolute separate spheres and work roles, based on their culture's definitions of "masculinity" and "femininity" or even on real physical differences, disobey biblical admonitions to neither add to nor subtract from its precepts (Deut. 4:2; Rev. 22:18–19). In doing so, they add unnecessary hardships to men's and women's lives.

The Bible's silences are there by God's design and wisdom. They allow flexibility, respecting the differences between individual men and women, different stages in the male and female life cycle, and different cultures and economies. They allow the flexibility needed in times of crisis, when unemployment, death, illness, or desertion strike a family. A brittle identification of women as homemakers and men as breadwinners adds unnecessary hardships to an already vulnerable family.

Difference and Equality in Marriage

Fox-Genovese quotes Paul's teaching about equality in Galatians 3:26–28. That text reads: "For in Christ Jesus you are all children of God through faith. As many of you as were baptized into Christ have clothed yourselves with Christ. There is no longer Jew or Greek, there is no longer slave or free, there is no longer male and female; for all of you are one in Christ Jesus" (NRSV). Reflecting on this passage, Fox-Genovese argues that it refers to our "equality before God's judgment and within his love," but that Paul "did not intend to transform the standing of and relations among people in the world." I would agree that the *primary* meaning of the text has to do with our relationship with God. The divisions and hierarchies of this world no longer have any bearing on our status before God. All who believe in Christ are one and share in the inheritance as children. But the New Testament is clear that this theological truth did indeed have profound equalizing implications for "relations among people in the world."

One of the main reasons for the Roman persecution of Christians was that the church challenged the rigid hierarchies and divisions of the Greco-Roman world. It is no accident that slaves and women of all classes, both married and single, became Christians in much greater numbers than free Roman males. They gained status and authority in the church, whereas for men, being "in Christ" meant relinquishing legal rights and privileges. It is no accident that the Christian church was largely responsible for the gradual undermining of slavery in the ancient world, beginning with Paul's subversive letter to Philemon. The church spearheaded the adoption of abandoned infants, provided financial support for their upbringing, and refused to stigmatize them as the Romans did because of their automatic legal status as slaves. The Christians knew that every believer is saved by adoption through the amazing reversal of God the Father, who abandoned his only Son to make our adoption possible. In other words, the equalizing of our status before God had profound, practical, day-to-day implications in the treatment of exposed infants "in this world."

More directly relevant to our discussion, the New Testament teaching on marriage challenged traditional, hierarchical Roman marriage at virtually every point. Christian marriage is a covenant between complementary equals. It is neither a one-sided, male-ruled dominion nor a brittle egalitarian contract. In Ephesians 5:21–33, the apostle Paul describes marriage as a mutual submission of husband and wife, a wholehearted 100-percent giving of each to the other throughout their lives. The wife's submission "in all things" is matched by the husband's sacrificial love "to the death," a love that can only take flesh as he submits his preferences to her good. A husband who loves his wife enough to die for her, as Christ loved and died for the church, must be willing to make much smaller and more likely sacrifices, like changing his career or not changing his career, or even changing a diaper! Paul made this very concrete by exhorting husbands to love their wives as they loved their own bodies, which they nourished and tenderly cared for. His love is for the purpose of her growth in glory, the development of her gifts, abilities, and character.

In comparing other New Testament teaching it is clear that the wife's submission no more means complying with every request of her husband than his willingness to die obligates him to die for any whim of his wife. Sapphira was rebuked by the apostle Peter and even lost her life for agreeing with her husband to lie (Acts 5:9). Both husband and wife are disciples of Jesus first, and their marriage obligations are subservient to their commitment to the Lord.

In 1 Corinthians 7 the apostle Paul equalizes the position of husbands and wives, subverting Roman law and custom in the process. He equalizes the Greco-Roman double sexual standard embodied in the marriage legislation of Emperor Augustus. Christian husbands and wives had then, and continue to have, an equal responsibility to avoid adultery and divorce. They also have the same divorce rights in cases of radical covenant breaking. Ironically, Christian sexual equality calls men to conform to women's "traditional" virtue, in contrast to individualistic feminist equality, which gives women the right to be as promiscuous as men.

Paul explicitly taught that husbands and wives have an equal responsibility to care for each other. He contrasted the advantages of vocational freedom for single men and women with the distractions of family commitments for both sexes (1 Cor. 7:32–35). In other words, the watershed for vocational freedom is marriage, not gender. This is not the picture of a wife as a subordinate satellite to her husband and his career with no real identity and vocation of her own. Paul assumed that both husbands and wives would make sacrifices of career, power, money, leisure, and freedom for the sake of each other and their children. This equality of responsibility to serve sacrificially does not come from an individualistic, contractual model of marriage. Rather, it is an expression of the mutual submission of committed, covenant marriage.

Nowhere in the New Testament's teaching about marriage and family is any particular "sanctified" division of labor spelled out. The Pauline metaphor of husband as head of his wife does not imply that men should earn all or most of the money. Fox-Genovese states that marriages in which men share domestic tasks with their wives and marriages in which men earn less than 50 percent of the family's income are more likely than "traditional" marriages to end in divorce. She also states that the more the wife earns, the more likely her husband is to abuse her. These statements raise serious questions about causation. It is by no means clear that the sharing of work roles and responsibilities is what causes a higher rate of divorce and abuse or that more "traditional" roles are the causative factor in greater marital stability. A correlation does not prove causation. There are too many factors, and the issues are much too complex. What kind of marriages were these? Within a secular, contractual model of marriage, in which both spouses demand their "individual rights," *no* particular division of labor is a safeguard against divorce or abuse. On the other hand, within the biblical model of committed, covenant marriage, any number of divisions of labor (from the most "traditional" to the most "nontraditional") can work without threatening the marriage. Again, equality is not necessarily tied to an uncommitted, contractual model of marriage.

The apostle Peter explicitly addressed the relationship between sexual difference and equality when he commanded Christian husbands to resist their culture's attitude, which exploited women's greater vulnerability (1 Peter 3:7). I suspect he was referring to the vulnerability inherent in bearing children and the socioeconomic vulnerability of women living in a sexist culture.[4] In other words, the greater vulnerability of women is in part creational and in part a result of the fall. This general power difference between men and women may well be what stands behind the Pauline metaphor of husband as head of his wife as Christ is head of the church (Eph. 5:23). The husband has a protective, servant-leadership responsibility for his wife in view of her greater vulnerability. Peter even warned Christian men that if they did not honor their wives as equal heirs of the gracious gift of life, God would not hear their prayers (1 Peter 3:7). This is a striking example of the Bible's ethic of power and the relationship between equality and difference. Those with greater power have no license to abuse those with less power. Instead, they are to protect, honor, and empower the weak.

Peter was applying the truth of Galatians 3:28 to the marriage relationship. Since men and women are on an equal footing before God—both undeserving recipients of the gift of life—men are not to see their greater power as evidence of superiority or privilege. Husbands are to live out the virtues of service and self-sacrifice toward their wives in costly ways. Roman law gave men absolute power over their wives and all household members. Following Christ meant willingly relinquishing those rights and privileges and serving family members as equals. Following Christ today has the same implications for anyone with power. Both men and women must be willing to relinquish rights in service of the more vulnerable, and specifically children.

Men and Women's Joint Stewardship of Children

Shared parenting—or "joint stewardship for children," as Fox-Genovese puts it—is the biblical norm. This pattern was established at creation and confirmed throughout the Old and New Testaments. In the Book of Proverbs, both fathers and mothers are admonished to love, teach, delight in, and discipline their children. The apostle Paul exhorted older women to teach the younger women how to love their husbands and children; and he warned fathers not to exasperate, embitter, or provoke their children to anger, but rather to nurture them in the training and instruction of the Lord (Eph. 6:4; Col. 3:21).

While we may assume that fathers' and mothers' contributions to child-rearing are complementary and not identical, the silence of the Bible is again striking. There is no delineation of separate maternal or paternal responsibilities, though there are many places where they could have been asserted had they been intended. I believe that silence is intentional. Aside from the obvious fact that only women can bear babies and nurse them, there is no particular "sanctified" transcultural child-rearing division of labor. There is room for flexibility in the ways fathers and mothers share their parenting and work responsibilities, depending on their individual gifts and temperaments, life situations, and culture and economy. Gender complementarity is not defined in terms of separate roles, responsibilities, activities, or attitudes—for example, that fathers should be financial providers and disciplinarians and mothers should be hands-on nurturers and comforters. It is more holistic, mysterious, and flexible. Because fathers and mothers complement each other, children need love, discipline, time, and intimate care from both.

The mistake conservatives often make is to absolutize what they call the "traditional" division of labor—man is the breadwinner and a woman's place is in the home raising children—as if God established and sanctioned that particular division of labor for all time. Women who work outside the home are accused of being selfish and abandoning their God-given roles. Family breakdown is blamed on them. In fact, there is nothing particularly biblical or traditional about that division of labor. It was *one way* of coping with the upheaval of industrialization and the consequent removal of economic work from the home. It was a middle-class ideal that has never been possible for the poor. In biblical times, as in all preindustrial societies, men and women literally raised bread and children together at home with a variety of divisions of labor.

John Demos, who has done pioneering work in the history of fatherhood, argues that in America, until about 1820, the father was considered the primary parent. Child-rearing advice books were addressed to fathers, and in custody cases, fathers invariably got custody of their children. It was believed that fathers understood their young better than mothers. While mothers had primary care of infants, older children were under their father's supervision and religious and moral education. Child care gradually came to be considered "women's work" from the 1820s on, as economic work increasingly left the home.[5] As work left the home for the first time, so did men. We should remember that historically fathers were the first to abandon home and children.

Fox-Genovese acknowledges that fathers' "contribution to children's lives is indispensable," and she states that it is "heartening" that "many fathers are assuming a growing responsibility for the household and the rearing of children." Nevertheless, the overwhelming weight of her argument, both explicitly and implicitly, is that motherhood is the special vocation of women in a way that fatherhood is not for men. Therefore, the impact of mothers on their children's lives is more significant and influential, both for good and bad. While she is careful not to blame women as individuals for the contemporary family crisis, she implies, often by innuendo, that today's pattern of mothers working outside the home is indicative of a rejection of women's special vocation and is therefore particularly harmful to children in a way that fathers working outside the home is not.

I could not agree more that "children would fare better . . . if *one* [my emphasis] of their parents were at home when the children return from school." In general, children today are being raised by themselves, their peers, and by electronic appliances. The consequences are catastrophic. It should be no surprise that children and teenagers get into the most serious trouble between 3:00 P.M. and 6:00 P.M. when they are at home alone. But Fox-Genovese's warnings are all connected to mothers working outside the home and do not include fathers' neglect or absence from their children's lives. This is in spite of the overwhelming documentation that irresponsible fathers are the cause of some of our most entrenched and growing social problems, for example, juvenile prisons full of fatherless boys with no impulse control.

Fox-Genovese refers to the argument that "men and women must equally work to restore the stability and vitality of families" as "superficially seductive," implying that it may sound persuasive but in reality "the argument for equality is deeply flawed." What exactly is it that she claims is "deeply flawed"? It is not the idea of equal responsibility but an individualistic, contractual idea of marriage that says, "I won't devote myself to children, husband, and family unless you do every bit as much as I do." I agree that any such individualistic bargaining is deeply flawed and that it is entirely inconsistent with Christian responsibility and character. But she is objecting to a model of the family that is diametrically opposed to committed, covenant marriage, in which mother and father share the responsibility of raising their children with flexibility and creativity. By confusing equal responsibility with contractual individualism, she misses the opportunity to encourage Christian couples to adopt a truly biblical model of the family, which could be a nonpolarizing force for family renewal in our time.

Positively, the growing fatherhood movement is an encouraging sign of the times, which Christians should applaud and wholeheartedly endorse. From all sides of the political spectrum, Christian and non-Christian men are waking up not only to the responsibility but also to the joys of hands-on fatherhood. Feminists, the secular men's movement, the Fatherhood Initiative (started by David Blankenhorn and others), Promise Keepers, and even conservative James Dobson (of Focus on the Family) are all calling fathers to a renewed, time-intensive, openly affectionate commitment to their children.

My husband and I have had the privilege of working with L'Abri Fellowship, a residential study center, during all of our child-rearing years. As we work together from home, we have had the freedom to share child care with great flexibility at every stage of our children's lives. Far more than a duty, this has been an enormous joy to both of us and to our children. I am convinced that the friendship our three grown sons have with their father has an enormous amount to do with the time he has spent with them since they were infants. They have grown up knowing that their dad loves and enjoys them and is genuinely interested in their thoughts, feelings, and interests. All three of them look forward to being hands-on fathers themselves, if and when they are blessed with children.

My brother is a pastor. When his children were young, his wife asked that he take over more of the child care to enable her to get her Ph.D. He agreed, and though he found the adjustment difficult at first, he has no doubt that it was one of the best decisions of his life. It is a joy to see the genuine friendship he and his wife now have with their two college-age children.

While my brother's family and mine have had more flexibility than most families have in today's economy, those parents who prioritize shared child-rearing are finding all kinds of creative ways to do it. This commitment needs to be enthusiastically encouraged rather than censured as a repudiation of gender roles.

Fox-Genovese rightly points out that the reason for the glass ceiling is not always sexist discrimination against women. Many women have different priorities and willingly forgo career advancement to spend time at home with their children. I recall a moving discussion in a class I audited several years ago on feminist theory, taught by Christina Hoff Sommers at Clarke University. She asked the students (all women except for one brave man) to describe their hopes for the future. Most of the women admitted rather sheepishly that they longed for the kind of marriage they could be certain would last and would give them the necessary financial security to raise their own children at home. One self-described "radical feminist" chastised the others vehemently, reminding them that they *had* to be economically self-sufficient to protect themselves from what had happened to their mothers. The others sighed in resigned agreement. Most of their mothers had quit jobs and stayed home to raise children, only to be deserted by husbands in their middle years and left in complete economic vulnerability. I found the entire discussion terribly poignant. It made me realize how essential committed marriage is to the very possibility of mothers or fathers being able to care for their own children at home.

In conclusion, what I have tried to show is that if we are going to encourage the strengthening of the family, especially in its care of children, we need to strengthen the marriage commitment itself. This is not something that wives and mothers can "make happen" alone. Christians can only exercise leadership in the renewal of committed, covenant marriage and family if both men and women repudiate individualism and the ideology of individual rights and work to restore the stability and vitality of families. God, give us grace to do this.

The Signs of Kuyper's Times, and of Ours

Response by Mary Stewart Van Leeuwen

Professor Elizabeth Fox-Genovese's "Women and the Future of the Family" is the fourth annual Kuyper Lecture sponsored by the Washington-based Center for Public Justice. I therefore wish to reflect on how Kuyper himself might have reacted to this lecture had he been a fly on the wall alongside the audience of late-twentieth-century people who came to hear it.

Mary Stewart Van Leeuwen is professor of psychology and philosophy at Eastern College in St. Davids, Pennsylvania, where she also is a resident scholar at the Center for Christian Women in Leadership. She received her Ph.D. at Northwestern University, Evanston, Illinois. A widely published writer, she is the author of *Gender and Grace* (InterVarsity Press, 1990). She is the coeditor of *Religion, Feminism, and the Family* (Westminster John Knox Press, 1996); and *After Eden: Facing the Challenge of Gender Reconciliation* (Eerdmans, 1993).

Points of Agreement

Fox-Genovese notes that we live in a time of great social
upheaval, and so too did Kuyper. Indeed, many of the trends
that she highlights were beginning to gather momentum a
century ago in Europe. The industrial revolution was caus-
ing economic dislocation and a steady exodus of people
from rural areas to cities. In addition, the longer, premod-
ern tradition of concrete and localized *responsibility* (to
family, to region, to religious duty) was giving way to an emphasis on abstract, individual *rights* in political, economic,
and legal arenas. Previously covenantal relationships, including marriage, were more and more seen as mere con-
tracts between individuals, and an increasingly complex
legal structure was needed to enforce them. Money was re-
placing kin and other social networks as the major economic safety net, and people competed both within and
across classes for more of it.

Kuyper was one of many late-nineteenth-century
thinkers who tried to grapple with the mixed implications
of these shifts. Others included Max Weber, Ernst Troeltsch,
and Otto Jellinek, all three of whom converged annually
with Kuyper at a spa in Switzerland for intense discussions
of social issues. In 1891, Pope Leo XIII issued his social en-
cyclical *Rerum Novarum,* in which he acknowledged the potential of modernity for improving standards of living and
giving the disenfranchised more voice but decried the economic injustices of unregulated capitalism and the individualist emphasis of liberal political thought.

Kuyper, like Leo XIII, was neither a Luddite nor a defender
of aristocratic privilege. Kuyper's strong view of common
grace—the idea that God restrains the scope of sin and works
not just through Christians but through whomever God
chooses—and his sensitivity to the Bible's prophetic voice for
justice allowed him to endorse much of the liberal project for
emancipating people—women included—from poverty, ignorance, and powerlessness.[1] Indeed, it is fair to say that he

was one of the early architects of the welfare state. At the same time, Kuyper rejected the French revolutionary concept of the individual as sovereign; in fact, his political party was called the Anti-Revolutionary Party. And he equally rejected the opposite, Hegelian notion that the state is the highest human authority. Instead, he developed—and bequeathed to those whom he influenced at the Center for Public Justice and elsewhere—the concept of *sphere sovereignty.*

At the root of this concept was Kuyper's concern for what he called the "organic" structures of social life. He vigorously defended the freedom of various spheres of activity (such as church, politics, family, business, education, labor, science, and art) each to develop its unique calling without being overwhelmed by the state, denied in pursuit of individual freedom, or reduced one to another among themselves. Today, we might say that Kuyper wanted to uphold a civil society of independent institutions that would not be destroyed by either atomistic individualism or state or corporate totalitarianism.

But for Kuyper these mediating institutions were not mere sociological constructs, nor were they completely voluntary. Rather, each aspect of this "associational diversity" had its own God-given character and authority. Nor was Kuyper alone among Christians in thinking this way. In *Rerum Novarum* Pope Leo XIII introduced a concept somewhat similar to sphere sovereignty—called *subsidiarity*—into Catholic social thought. Kuyper contrasted sphere sovereignty with the twin distortions of individualism and statism when he spoke to an American audience in 1898 as follows:

> [In] the French revolution . . . the sovereign God is dethroned and man [*sic*] with his free will is placed on the vacant seat. It is the will of man which determines all things. . . . Thus one comes from the individual man to the many men; and in those many men conceived as *the people* there is supposedly hidden the deepest fountain of all sovereignty. There is no question of a sovereignty derived from God, which He, under certain conditions, implants in the people. . . . It is a

sovereignty of the people, therefore, which is perfectly identical with atheism. . . .

[By contrast], we do not conceive of society as a conglomerate, but as analyzed in its organic parts, to honor, in each of these parts, the independent character which appertains to them. . . . In a Calvinistic sense we understand that the family, business, science, art and so forth are all social spheres, which do not owe their existence to the state . . . but obey a high authority within their own bosom; an authority which rules, by the grace of God, just as the authority of the State does.[2]

So what, for Kuyper, was the God-given "organic" character of family life? "From the duality of man and woman," he wrote, "marriage arises. From the original existence of *one* man and *one* woman monogamy comes forth. The children exist by reason of the innate power of reproduction. In all this there is nothing mechanical. The development is spontaneous, just as that of the stem and the branches of a plant."[3] This may sound like a very un-Calvinist appeal to natural theology, but Kuyper's sense of pervasive depravity qualifies it even as he maintains an organic view of the family based in God's creation:

True, sin here also has exerted its disturbing influence and has distorted much which was intended as a blessing into a curse. But this fatal efficiency of sin has been stopped by common grace. Free love may try to dissolve, and concubinage to desecrate, the holiest tie as it pleases; but for the vast majority of our race, marriage remains the foundation of human society and the family retains its position as the primordial sphere in sociology.[4]

Clearly, Kuyper, as our imaginary fly on the wall, would find echoes of sphere sovereignty in Fox-Genovese's lecture. She too is concerned that the liberation of the individual and the worldwide spread of capitalism have weakened "the family understood as a kind of corporate enclave . . . distinct from other institutions or associations." As one example of this she cites America's current legal defense of abortion in terms of "the privacy of the individual [woman] rather than the privacy of the family." As a result, men are effectively disenfranchised from having any voice in reproductive decisions unless their wives or lovers choose to include them. She further notes that this kind of sexual individualism contributes to the view of children as commodities to be retained or disposed of at will, rather than "a familial and social responsibility," and astutely observes, "It should make us thoughtful that, on this point, the large business interests and the feminist activists agree."

This is conceptual language that Kuyper would recognize and affirm. In terms of sphere sovereignty, a family is not a business to be evaluated purely in terms of costs and benefits to its individual shareholders. Nor does it convey license either for men to dominate women or for women to turn men, if they so wish, into mere sperm donors. It is a covenantal union of two persons, each made in the image of God, who together share the potential to procreate children who are themselves made in God's image. In creation, marriage was and is meant to be a blessing, but like all other spheres of human life it is marred by sin and is thus subject to the famous Protestant principle of *semper reformanda*. Thus, Kuyper's Calvinism condemned "not merely all open slavery and systems of caste, but also covert slavery of women." He further exhorted Christians in all spheres of life to use their "character or talent . . . [not] for self-aggrandizement or ambitious pride, but for the sake of spending it in the service of God."[5] This too finds echoes in Fox-Genovese. She affirms the past work feminists have done to reduce women's vulnerability within marriage but also chides contemporary feminists who call on women to reject the biblical virtues of service and sacrifice in the family. These virtues, she reminds us, are among the personality ideals of the generic Christian regardless of sex, and no marriage or family can survive without them.

At the turn of the last century, divorce and nonmarital cohabitation were rarer than they are now, though Kuyper was aware that both were on the rise in Europe. As an intellectual Christian who appealed to empirical data to support his own theories, he would have listened with interest to Fox-Genovese's summary of research on the results of our own culture's decades-long tolerance of divorce and sexual freedom. For despite differing political allegiances, social scientists now generally agree that divorce and nonmarital parenthood—even after controlling for the effects of any accompanying financial hardship—have enduring, negative consequences for both children and adults. Divorce, it appears, is not the panacea for adults in unhappy marriages that many assumed it would be thirty years ago. No social scientist denies that it may be the lesser of two evils in cases of chronic abuse, adultery, addiction, or financial irresponsibility. But data collected since the 1970s show that, on the whole, marriage is associated with enhanced well-being for both wives and husbands, as compared to divorced, widowed, cohabiting, or never-married persons. On average, and controlling for age, class, and education, they have better health, more wealth, and higher earnings. They even report—popular myths to the contrary—more physical and emotional satisfaction with sex than sexually active singles or cohabiting couples.[6]

Points of Disagreement

So far I have concentrated on aspects of Fox-Genovese's lecture with which Kuyper would agree and which I, as a neo-Kuyperian, firmly endorse. But if Kuyper were a fly on the wall, he would also find some aspects of her lecture less than totally to his liking. For one thing, he endorsed a much stronger view of the doctrine of separate spheres for men and women than she appears to do. For example, Fox-Genovese is concerned that many American women, captive to a legalistic unisex mentality, resist taking time out from the waged workforce to care for children unless their husbands respond exactly in kind. But nowhere does she suggest that women would function best as women if they did not have access to the vote or to professions such as politics, law, or university teaching, or that men should never be involved in the care of young children. Kuyper, however, was convinced that a Christian understanding of sphere sovereignty required all of these restrictions. Let me elaborate a little.[7]

To begin with, Kuyper viewed the family as the most basic and irreducible of the creational spheres. Consequently, the idea of "one person, one vote" was to him an unwarranted intrusion of French Revolution–inspired individualism into an area of life that should be treated as an organic whole. As a result, he did not endorse a universal franchise but only one limited to heads of households. This in effect meant only husbands, though Kuyper conceded that widows, as surviving heads of households, should also be allowed to vote, but only as long as they remained unmarried. It also meant, for Kuyper, that as long as adult children—of whatever age—lived under their parents' roof, they too should not have the franchise.

In the second place, especially as he grew older, Kuyper became more certain not just that family, business, politics, and the academy were sovereign spheres with their own character and rights but that certain people belonged naturally and by divine decree to certain spheres—namely, women to the family and men to all the others mentioned:

> The private and public life form two separate spheres, each with their own way of existing, with their own task. [And] those two kinds of gifts, at least as a rule, seem to fall along the lines of the natural distinction between man and woman. . . . And it is on the basis of this state of affairs, which has not been invented by us, but which God himself has imposed on us, that in public life the woman does not stand equally with the man. No more than it can be said of the man that in married life he has been called to also achieve in the family that which is achieved by the woman.[8]

In actual practice, Kuyper showed great concern for public justice when it came to women. As a parliamentarian in the late 1880s, he supported the Netherlands' first general labor law, which restricted the hours women and children could work in factories. During his term as prime minister, he proposed legislation for workmen's insurance that included widows' pensions. He took for granted that working-class single women would enter domestic service, and he grudgingly tolerated middle-class single women supporting themselves in retail and clerical positions. But for him none of these practices were normative. To Kuyper most were the regrettable result of young men's preference for pursuing wealth and leading wild lives, rather than marrying and building a home for wife and family. "The woman's position of honor," he wrote in 1914, "is most effectively maintained if she can sparkle in private life, and in the public domain, for which the man is the appointed worker, she will never be able to fulfill anything but a subordinate role, in which her inferiority would soon come to light anyway."[9]

For Kuyper, women's "subordinate role" in public life permitted them limited participation, under male authority, in areas he saw as natural extensions of domesticity: orphanages, public health, nursery schools, and some forms of philanthropy. But women's entry into intellectual or political activity, he believed, would almost certainly unsex them. About the former he wrote:

> It is precisely this one-sided intellectual world that breaks the harmony in the feminine nature, which, glittering in her inner emotional richness, will tolerate no supremacy of the intellect. . . . Man and woman are fundamentally different in kind, and whoever has man take his place at the cradle and woman at the lectern makes life unnatural.[10]

And about political activity he wrote:

> It can never be maintained that the high authority in public life could be partly diverted from the man and carried over

to the woman. . . . In the public arena it finally comes down to the sword . . . and for that side of life the All-disposing Creator and Master of our life did not give special gifts to women.[11]

But this wholesale endorsement of the nineteenth-century doctrine of gendered separate spheres is inconsistent on Kuyper's part for two reasons. First of all, in no other respect does Kuyper go beyond describing sphere sovereignty in terms of various *life activities* to identifying certain spheres with certain *categories of people*. For example, there is no evidence in Kuyper's writings that racial groups (and the activities that make up their common stereotypes) constitute permanent, separate spheres as he understood that term. That is what Afrikaner Calvinists—many of them trained at Kuyper's Free University of Amsterdam—tried to claim during the development and hegemony of Apartheid. But Kuyperian Calvinists have long agreed that the doctrine of separate racial groups was a gross distortion of the idea of sphere sovereignty. Spheres have to do with specialized, organic types of activity—art, business, worship, education, science, family life, and so on. They do not refer to biologically marked groups of people.[12]

Yet when it came to the sexes, Kuyper showed himself to be less a Kuyperian and more a classic Victorian bourgeois thinker. For most of history, economically speaking, marriage has been a partnership between spouses, for whom workplace, dwelling place, and child-rearing space usually coincided, with a fair amount of flexibility in gender roles. Indeed, this was still the case for many of Kuyper's most loyal followers, who included many farm and small business families. Yet Kuyper somehow convinced himself that the doctrine of separate spheres—women as "angels of the home," men as "captains of industry" (and everything else)—was an unchanging historical and biblical given.

Kuyper's embrace of the doctrine of separate spheres for women and men is all the more puzzling in that it side-

stepped another durable Calvinist principle that in other re-
spects he fully embraced, namely, the *cultural mandate,*
which is foundational to the whole idea of sphere sovereignty. Kuyper and his followers advanced the idea of the
cultural mandate in order to challenge a dichotomous
thought pattern shared by many Christian pietists, namely,
the assumption that certain spheres of human functioning
(such as prayer, devotions, and religious study and observance) were "sacred" while others (such as science, politics,
business, and family) were "secular" and therefore of sec-
ondary importance to the Christian life or even detrimental
to it. By contrast, Kuyper insisted that all of life's activities
were blessed by God in creation and were to be developed
and redeemed according to norms that could be discerned
in Scripture.

But where does the idea of the cultural mandate origi-
nate? Calvinists without exception point to the biblical account of creation, but particularly Genesis 1:26–28:

> Then God said, "Let us make humankind in our image, ac-
> cording to our likeness; and let them have dominion over
> the fish of the sea, and over the birds of the air, and over the
> cattle, and over all the wild animals of the earth, and over
> every creeping thing that creeps upon the earth." So God
> created humankind in his own image, in the image of God he
> created them; male and female he created them. God blessed
> them, and God said to them, "Be fruitful and multiply, and
> fill the earth and subdue it; and have dominion over the fish
> of the sea and over the birds of the air and over every living
> thing that moves upon the earth." (NRSV)

Whatever else we may conclude about the image of God
from this passage, it seems clear that *accountable dominion,*
or stewardship, over the earth is one part of that image, and
accountable sociability—the call to form families and communities within and across generations—is another. But
note well: God does not say to the first woman, "Be fruitful
and multiply," and to the first man, "Subdue the earth."

Both mandates are given to both members of the primal pair, notwithstanding Kuyper's determination to specialize each by sex.

Moreover, the lesson of history (and Kuyper was big on drawing lessons from history) seems to be that when either mandate is grossly distorted, trouble eventually results. Thus, we should not be surprised that data collected during the past thirty years of increasing divorce and sexual libertarianism show that both are damaging to the well-being of children and adults. But neither should we be surprised that the extreme bifurcation of the cultural mandate by sex in nineteenth- and twentieth-century America eventually led to two successive waves of feminism aimed at overturning it. On this latter point it is important to note that the health advantages of marriage for women only began to equal those for men after the gains of second-wave feminism gave them more flexibility to combine domesticity with waged work, if they so desired.[13]

Sexual Difference and Human Equality

Fox-Genovese has shown awareness of both these distortions in her lecture, but she is generally more critical of women's distortions of the "fruitful and multiply" part of the mandate than of those that distort God's call to both sexes to "subdue the earth." In one sense this is understandable. Fox-Genovese criticizes today's establishment feminists, as do I, for their casual attitudes toward unborn life and heterosexual monogamy, and for the simplistic assumption by many of them that male sexism is the original sin and women are the virtually sinless victims of it. She is talking bluntly, woman to women, about women's own failures and responsibilities in family life, just as the male leaders of the Promise Keepers organization talk bluntly to men about theirs. But it is one thing to point out that the family as a creational sphere is under duress, that father absence is not improved by adding mother absence, and that all Christians are called to self-sacrifice as well as to personal vocational development. It is quite another to suggest, as she does toward the end of her lecture, that those—myself included—who support less differentiated gender roles and a reversal of the doctrine of separate spheres have substituted feminist individualism for "a Christian understanding of sexual difference and human equality."

The truth of the matter is that there is no single, clear understanding of sexual difference and equality that can be turned into a litmus test of Christian orthodoxy. Witness, for example, how much Fox-Genovese's own views on this subject differ from those of Abraham Kuyper, who was convinced that "God himself" had established that women should neither vote nor hold political office, let alone become university professors. Orthodox Christians ought not to disagree about things such as the Apostles' Creed or the importance of the Ten Commandments and the fruits of the Spirit. They can, and do, disagree over things such as whether people should be baptized as infants or adults, whether the church should be organized in a hierarchical or a parliamentary or a congregational fashion, how the sacrament of communion really works, and how much distinction in roles and status should exist between men and women.

Thus Bill McCartney, the founder and CEO of Promise Keepers, happily accepts women as ordained clergy but insists that the Bible calls for male headship in the family. Conversely, Pope John Paul II rejects gender hierarchy in marriage while continuing to deny that women can serve as priests in the church. Which one is right? In North American evangelicaldom, there are two opposing parachurch organizations with an equally high view of Scripture. One, the Council on Biblical Manhood and Womanhood, argues for male headship in both church *and* family. The other, Christians for Biblical Equality, argues that the responsibilities of leadership in *both* church and home should be distributed on the basis of gifts, expertise, and availability, not sex. Each organization has the support of well-trained biblical scholars working with accepted evangelical and reformational principles of exegesis. Which one is right?

In the church, as in politics, an old aphorism needs to be recalled: In essentials, unity; in nonessentials, liberty; in all things, charity. Calvinists of all people need to remember such principles: During the Reformation they used to drown Anabaptists who disagreed with them over the issue of infant baptism! In practice, most Christians settle the debate about gender roles simply by voting with their feet. And so Fox-Genovese has found her way into the Catholic Church, while I sit on the Board of Reference of Christians for Biblical Equality, even as I remain in a fence-sitting denomination that lets its individual districts decide whether or not to ordain women.

But even as we make these choices and argue for them, it is important not to suggest that those who disagree with us have not done their homework and are simply following the drumbeat of anti-Christian sentiment. For one thing, as Kuyper himself would be the first to point out, the reality of common grace means that God gets God's work done through whomever God chooses. Thus, the dividing line between "Christians and lions" is not as sharp as culture-war polarizers would like to believe. "Sometimes," Kuyper once wrote, "the world does better than expected and the church, worse."[14]

In addition, when we are tempted to elevate nonessential differences to the status of litmus tests for orthodoxy, we contribute to a culture-war mentality that reduces the possibility of fruitful dialogue. It is significant that Kuyper, despite his strong—and publicly voiced—differences with Catholics on certain doctrinal matters, was able to cooperate with them politically to set up a school system in the Netherlands, which, until this day, allows tax dollars to follow children to the school of their parents' confessional choice, whether Christian or not. Without trying to turn the

Netherlands into a theocracy, he insisted that worldviews shape all aspects of societal participation and that a just government should therefore recognize (and support proportionately) the civil-society activities of all groups, both religious and secular. It is in this tradition of "public justice" that his American descendants at the Center for Public Justice work to this day.

Three Models of Gender and Family Relations

This brings me to my final observation. It is odd that, in a lecture sponsored by a pubic policy organization, Fox-Genovese has no specific public policy recommendations to make in light of her concerns about the family. Yet much public policy discussion and experimentation are taking place on these issues worldwide, not all of it blindly catering to the distortions of establishment feminism that she deplores. There are three main models of gender and family relations competing for hegemony in the twenty-first century. Fox-Genovese and I would probably agree in rejecting the first two, but I believe the third represents a compromise we can both accept.[15]

To begin with, there are the forces of patriarchal reaction that aim to reinstate varying degrees of male headship and a highly gendered public-private dichotomy. Currently this option is most dramatically exemplified in the parts of Afghanistan under control of the Muslim Taliban movement. Under its sway, women are caught in an assortment of no-win dilemmas. They are banned from working in the public arena, even if they are war widows and the sole support of their children. They cannot be treated by male doctors, yet only a few women doctors from pre-Taliban days are allowed to continue practicing. They can no longer attend school or university and must be veiled and accompanied by a male relative when in public or risk suffering physical violence. Although the Taliban rhetoric is that women are better off under its system—protected by male relatives and rulers from the cultural and moral anarchy of the West—the reality is an extreme distortion of the cultural mandate, and one that accords neither with Muslim nor Afghan tradition. It is an attempt to turn the tragedy of fallen gender relations as expressed in Genesis 3:16 ("Your desire shall be for your husband, and he shall rule over you" [NRSV]) into an ethically normative and legally fixed pattern.

At the other extreme is the model Fox-Genovese criticizes, that of functional equality between the sexes. This model draws on the tradition of liberal individualism and is most fully implemented in the Scandinavian countries. It rejects all divisions of labor by sex as accidents of socialization that disadvantage women in particular and celebrates waged labor as women's only route to self-determination. It also devalues domestic activities, seeing them as tedious necessities to be evenly divided between partners or absorbed into an infrastructure of services done by third parties. Finally, it asserts that the individual rather than the couple or family should be the focus of welfare policy, whether for purposes of taxation, public pensions, or health benefits.

Thus, in Sweden working parents can receive state-subsidized day care to a total of almost $12,000 per year but cannot choose to take this subsidy as a cash grant to enable one or both of them to care for their children at home. Efforts to change this have been blocked by members of the Social Democrat Party who claim that any other practice would lead to the re-imprisonment of women in domesticity. This model for gender and family relations may be lightyears away from the Taliban's, but it is hardly a mark of liberation for women—or men either—to be shunted from one set of restrictive options to an opposite but equally confining one. The functional-equality model, though it uses the classical liberal language of individual freedom, is at least as restrictive as the older patriarchal model in its pressure to make all families operate in the same way.

The third, a "social-partnership" model, challenges the individualism and one-size-fits-all rigidity of the functional-equality approach while taking care to ensure that any marital division of labor does not render one spouse more vulnerable than the other. Instead of tax-subsidized day care on a take-it-or-leave-it basis, this model calls for direct cash subsidies or refundable tax credits either to replace the wages of a stay-at-home parent or to pay for child care supplied by others. (So far Finland is the only Western democracy that allows such a choice.) With regard to retirement income, the partnership model calls for all public and private pension accounts to be "credit-shared" between spouses. Such a practice may be incidental in marriages that last a lifetime, but it provides an important safety net in cases of divorce in which one spouse has fewer economic assets as a result of having been out of the waged workforce doing family work. (Thus far only Canada and Germany have versions of this policy as federal law.)

Finally, the social-partnership model is generally neutral as to how couples divide waged work and domestic responsibilities. But its supporters acknowledge that time taken out of the waged labor force by either spouse will reduce any pension account that depends on accumulated time in the workforce. Thus, in addition to credit-shared pensions, advocates of this model call for homemakers' pension credits covering the years spent in non-waged domestic activity. In the most common model, public pension retirement benefits that cease to accumulate during years of unpaid domestic activity are at least partially made up for by government contributions. Their accumulation might be left in the pension account for retirement, used for further education when a homemaker is ready to return to school, or used as capital to begin a business venture. Among the industrialized nations, Austria, Britain, France, and Hungary have institutionalized homemakers' pensions, varying in the amount that can be credited and the eligibility of persons by sex.

In the United States, we are a long way from approximating anything like the social-partnership model. But if it were to be implemented, it would address one of Fox-Genovese's concerns, namely, women's reluctance "to put a career temporarily on hold if they have reason to think that they—and their children—may have to depend on their salary" if the marriage does not survive. And we need also to recall that the countries that have implemented aspects of the social-partnership model also have national health care systems. If a homemaker is completely dependent on a spouse's work-based health insurance, that is another disincentive to take time out for child-rearing in a society as divorce-prone as our own.

It might well be that under such policies more women than men *would* opt for full or partial domesticity in the period when their children are young. I would see that as a completely acceptable outcome, provided that the policies themselves allowed men the same options for families who decide to do otherwise. As I have written elsewhere, I believe the most pressing issue today regarding family life is this: How can we put children first, without putting women last, and without putting men on the sidelines? In other words, how can we honor children's need for stable, nurturing families without reappropriating the dubious doctrine of separate spheres for women and men?[16]

In terms of public policy, I believe—and I hope Professor Fox-Genovese will agree—that something like the social-partnership model is at least part of the answer to that question. Had he lived longer, I think that Kuyper himself might have realized that just as it is uncreational and unjust to identify certain racial groups with different activities, so it is possible to maintain family integrity and a communitarian mind-set without the rigid gender specialization he too often defended. The challenge for his Christian followers, at the Center for Public Justice and elsewhere, will be to take Kuyper's valuable concept of sphere sovereignty and find ways to apply it justly in an increasingly global society. The shape of gender and family justice will understandably be somewhat different in different settings, depending on their degree of modernization and a host of other factors. But in every case, I think we can agree to agree on two things and work to persuade others of their importance. The first is the sphere sovereignty of family life, especially in a culture such as ours that routinely allows it to be compromised by forces such as individualism and consumerism. The second is the recognition that the cultural mandate is indeed a human mandate, not to be divided by ethnicity, gender, or class but shared by all who are made in the image of God.

Conclusion

James W. Skillen and Michelle N. Voll

Elizabeth Fox-Genovese, Stanley Grenz, Mardi Keyes, and Mary Stewart Van Leeuwen have illumined many important issues that now dominate public discussion of women and families in contemporary society. The disagreements among them only help to highlight the importance of the task facing Christians today of developing a well-grounded and sufficiently comprehensive perspective on women, the family, and public life. At least three things seem clear from their presentations.

First, the modern individualist, autonomy gospel cannot lead to justice for women, children, and families any more than it has led to justice for men. Not only does the elevation of the ideal of individual autonomy conflict with the biblical witness, it appears to be implicated in, if not the chief cause of, many contemporary social deformities.

Second, the family cannot be reduced to or accounted for in terms of a contract made by autonomous individuals.

The injustice to children—whether born or unborn—becomes evident all too quickly, but it is not only children who suffer. The meaning of a loving union—a covenant bond—between husband and wife cannot be disclosed or sustained by a purely contractual form of relationship in which each of the partners seeks his or her individual self-advancement and self-protection.

And third, a Christian approach to the proper recognition and treatment of women, children, and men must be grounded in the assumptions that human beings—male and female—are created in the image of God, made for a relationship with God, and called to mutual service for the glory of God and for the strengthening of each person through community with others.

Within this context of agreement, the question that appears to be most in dispute among our authors is this: What is *legitimate* about the historical differentiation of women's roles and responsibilities in all areas of God's creation regardless of the misdirected interpretations and malformations of those roles and responsibilities that have been advanced by radical feminists, certain business interests, and modern philosophical individualism generally?

Elizabeth Fox-Genovese emphasizes the negative, destructive consequences of feminist individualism: the legalization of abortion and the dismembering of the family in the name of enhancing individual autonomy. Although she does not argue for a return to an earlier era, her argument implies that the liberation of women from family service may have come at too great a cost to society and to Christian virtue. She urges Christians not to support the liberation of women on the basis of secular humanist autonomy claims.

The respondents agree with Fox-Genovese that humanist individualism is mistaken and no friend of biblical Christianity, but they worry that Fox-Genovese underestimates the negative features of a social order in which women are confined to the roles of wife and mother. Keyes and Van

Leeuwen in particular point to an unresolved ambiguity in the fact that Fox-Genovese apparently approves of many aspects of the modern liberation of women (far beyond that accepted by Abraham Kuyper, for example) but is reluctant to ground that approval in a positive, Christian affirmation of the equality of men and women.

Grenz and Keyes argue that the Bible affirms the equal dignity and worth of both men and women. Moreover, it does so in ways that both honor family life, with its mutual obligations, and reject the generalized subordination of women to men in public and private life. Thus, from their point of view, the urgent need of the moment is not only for Christians to oppose the dangers of radical feminism but to develop the kinds of relationships in both the family and the broader society that will allow women as well as men to exercise their God-given capabilities and responsibilities. Women and men together need to develop the full meaning of the image of God and fulfill all the responsibilities of the image of God.

Four Necessary Commitments

Positive, forward movement on these issues from a Christian point of view would seem to require at least four simultaneous commitments.

1. First, as Van Leeuwen, Grenz, and Keyes emphasize, God's cultural mandate to Adam and Eve, recorded in Genesis—including both procreation and the social-cultural development of creation—was given to the man and the woman together, to the image of God, male and female. The Bible does not teach that God intended women and men permanently to fill only certain distinct roles in society. The clear difference between man and woman, sexually speaking, identifies the woman and not the man as child-bearer and birth-giver. However, neither that fact nor biblical instruction leads to the conclusion that at all times and in all

places only men should be public officials and only women should care for young children, or that only women should oversee family households during the day and only men should bring home economic support from outside employment. Women and men together bear the image of God and have received the cultural mandate; together they need to use all of their gifts to serve God in all the ways God has called them to do so.

2. This means, in the second place, that being a man or a woman does not mean finding the full meaning of one's life in only one or two roles. A man is not exhaustively defined or fulfilled by the role of husband or father. Neither is a woman exhaustively defined or fulfilled by the role of wife or mother. Some men and women may never marry. Others may marry and choose to confine their labors, at least for a time, largely to the responsibilities of family life. Still others may marry and continue to exercise responsibilities beyond their roles as husband or wife. Especially in view of the high degree of differentiation of contemporary society, in which many people in a country such as the United States have the opportunity to exercise a wide range of diverse responsibilities, it would be strange to imagine that equally well-educated, equally gifted men and women should not both develop their talents in art or industry, in politics or philanthropy, in education or gardening.

3. Thus, in the third place, the question for Christians, it would appear, is not whether women should be confined to fewer responsibilities than men, but rather whether both men and women will fully accept and exercise the responsibilities incumbent upon them when they do take up various responsibilities and enter certain roles. For example, from a biblical point of view, no person may escape the responsibility of being a son or a daughter in relation to one's parents. There are exceptions, of course, such as when children are not raised by their parents or when parents die young and leave their children without responsibility for them. Yet for most of us, no matter how many other roles we may

have, we may not be excused for failing to fulfill our responsibilities toward our parents. By contrast, many other responsibilities may be freely undertaken. One need not marry. And as the apostle Paul admonished, there may be good reason for some Christians not to do so. A woman as well as a man may choose not to marry precisely in order to fulfill some calling that might be incompatible with marriage and family life.

From a Christian point of view, if a couple *does* enter into marriage, both husband and wife are to accept all the obligations of marriage and mutual service to one another. That may mean having to relinquish other responsibilities or to forgo some other interest, the exercise of which is incompatible with their marriage. Likewise, if children are born to a couple, the roles of father and mother bring additional, inescapable responsibilities, and these might further confine both parents at least during the child-rearing years. The direction of Christian argument, as Keyes emphasizes, ought to be that both father and mother, in mutual service to one another and to their children, will give themselves to the enrichment of each member of the family. It is wrong, in other words, to say that if fathers can be relatively free of child-rearing responsibilities while fully employed outside the home, then mothers should aim to be equally free of child-rearing responsibilities while being fully employed outside the home. Normatively speaking, a husband and wife, a mother and father should be related in a union of mutual service so that within the financial limits that are theirs they will balance marriage, child-rearing, employment, and other opportunities and responsibilities to the benefit of all members of the family. Insofar as the raising of children is a first priority, it should not be at the sacrifice of the mother only. Neither mother nor father, neither children nor parents should be guided by an individualistic, egalitarian ideal that drives the marriage partners away from each other, and both of them away from their children.

While marriage and family are unique, widely encompassing, highly demanding, and more-than-contractual relationships, the kinds of decisions marriage partners and parents need to make are not entirely unlike the kinds of decisions they make when they accept other obligations that also restrict or prohibit their acceptance of yet additional ones. Think, for example, of the university professor who accepts a position in government, or the businessperson who accepts a time-consuming responsibility on the board of directors of a service organization. Accepting one obligation may mean relinquishing or cutting back on another. No person can expect to do and be everything that humans can do and be. The image of God is not only male and female but also multigenerational, numbering in the billions. We bear human responsibilities in a vast network of communities, not as lone individuals, each of whom has to try to become and do everything humanly possible. The answer, in part, to Fox-Genovese's criticism of parental irresponsibility, fostered by radical feminism, is to reassert the Christian message of liberation in Christ that calls Christ's followers to accept gladly their bond-servant obligations to God and to one another with the talents and decisions and opportunities that each has. And this message of liberation holds for men as well as women, for husbands as well as wives, for fathers as well as mothers.

4. Finally, to affirm the legitimacy of diverse human responsibilities shared by both men and women need not be incompatible with the affirmation that every person should enjoy the same rights of citizenship and equal standing before the law. In other words, equal civil/political rights for individuals need not be grounded in an individualistically reductionist ideology. Equal civil rights and legal treatment are owed to each citizen as part of the responsibilities and rights of membership in the political community. The political or civic community is one of the many institutions in which people bear responsibilities and should enjoy the benefits of membership. Consequently, civil rights should

not be interpreted by citizens or by Supreme Court justices to mean that individual autonomy should always trump associational obligations. Every individual should have a right to marriage, but marriage should not be reduced in law to nothing more than a contract between individuals. Every adult citizen (and not only men, or only property owners, or only white people) should have the right to vote, but voters should not be treated as only individuals, unencumbered by a variety of other associational responsibilities. Every child should be assured of government's protection of his or her life, but this does not give government or the courts the right to redefine the family as nothing more than a collection of individuals. The rights of the family, just as the rights of churches and of other institutions, organizations, and associations, also need to be protected under the law of the civic community. Thus, no citizen should be compelled by government to join or not join a church. But churches should enjoy the right to shape their communions and enjoin obligations on their members in ways not dictated by the state.

One of the relatively healthy characteristics of the American legal and political system is that it acknowledges the civil rights of every individual citizen while not claiming that government has totalitarian responsibility to govern the affairs internal to every human relationship and institution. Human persons are always more than citizens and more than merely individuals. Fox-Genovese, Mary Ann Glendon, and others are correct to warn us about the dangers of an individualist mode of legal and political reasoning that, even now, is threatening to dismember families into mere collections of individuals, to set children over against their parents, and to set spouses against one another in ways that weaken parental, spousal, and other social responsibilities. The answer to this deformity, however, is not to question the legitimacy of individual civil rights but to affirm the nonexclusive and nonreductionist character of those rights, which must be held in balance with the rights of the family and other institutions.

Public Policy Concerns

If these four affirmations or commitments help lay the foundation for forward movement on gender and family justice, then there are a variety of public policy concerns that come to the fore for an organization such as the Center for Public Justice. Public policy concerns are not the only, and may not be the first, priority of Christians struggling with questions of justice for women, children, and families. Moreover, from the viewpoint of the Center, not every matter of gender concern should come under government's authority. Least of all should government be allowed by its lawmaking authority to displace or weaken the spousal, parental, and occupational responsibilities that belong to people who are always more than citizens.

Nevertheless, there are important matters of governmental responsibility that call for our attention, including both the way government recognizes and protects individuals and families (as well as other institutions) and the way government's social, economic, and welfare policies bear on individuals, institutions, and organizations. These are the matters of particular concern to the Center, which is a public policy and civic education organization, not a church, business, school, social service organization, or family counseling center. Christian citizens should be at the forefront of reforming public laws that do not adequately deal with men, women, and children in a society that has constructively opened up more and more opportunities for everyone but that has increasingly been shaped by the dogma of secularist individualism.

In her book *Care and Equality: Inventing a New Family Politics* (Knopf, 1999), Mona Harrington contends that those who have helped create a society in which more and more women have entered the workforce outside the home bear an obligation to address the resulting "caretaking crisis." Harrington does not challenge the individualistic assumptions that undergird the crisis, but she urges those who share her assumptions not to ignore the fact that care for children and the elderly was once provided largely by stay-at-home moms. The society we now have requires a new politics—a new way of thinking about public policy—because until recently, public policies took for granted that caretaking would occur in homes in which one spouse or parent (usually the wife or mother) was present during the day. Those of us who do not accept individualist assumptions for human society and public policy making have an even more important responsibility to rethink government's responsibility—both to hold on to good laws and to reform bad laws.

Among the most important laws and policies that bear on women and children are those that deal with the family as an institution. But in order for government to recognize and protect marriage and the family it must first identify them properly. This is the juncture at which basic suppositions are so important. If the law is grounded in individualistic assumptions, then marriage and family are viewed as nothing more than contractual relationships among individuals. If, on the other hand, the law is grounded in the assumption that humans are constituted through social relationships, communities, and institutions, then those relationships, communities, and institutions themselves must be taken into account by the law. Therefore, every aspect of the law and public policy that bears on the identification or misidentification, the recognition or nonrecognition of marriage and family are of first importance. This matter of proper identification and recognition touches many if not most policies, ranging from education to employment, family to taxes, the economy to welfare.

Think, for example, of government's tax policies. Americans are used to federal and state tax deductions for dependent care. These deductions are a way of recognizing the need of families for more income during the years of child raising but also the value of elder care and the care of other adult dependents. If we are concerned about families holding together, then we should consider how much the amount of this deduction should be increased, along with an increase in the earned income tax credit (EITC) for lower-income working families who have the same responsibilities of child-rearing but not enough income to be able to benefit from a tax deduction. Additional uses of the tax code to benefit families can also be envisioned, as can direct child care payments as is done in some other countries.

When it comes to public financial support for child care, there is also the question of what government takes into consideration. Many proponents of either tax deductions for or direct government subsidy of child care take into account only child care that is purchased outside the home, as Van Leeuwen points out. Public subsidy of only this kind of child care, however, puts increased pressure on family income, making it less and less possible for families with only one income-earning spouse to survive. For government to protect families and not simply to foster out-of-the-home employment of both mothers and fathers, it should provide the same child care tax deductions, tax credits, or direct subsidies to families who take care of their children at home.

Beyond the use of tax codes and public disbursements targeted at families and child care, there are also legal measures that are now being taken, and in most cases should be taken, to make divorce a more deliberate and extended process, giving spouses more time to reconcile and to count the great cost that may befall them and their children if they go through with a divorce. Here again, the question is whether marriage should be treated more like a voluntary business contract or as having enduring, constitutive meaning for its members. Moreover, there is a significant challenge today to overcome the vastly greater social and economic harm done to women compared to men in many if not most divorce cases. Van Leeuwen suggests, for example, that in addition to instituting "credit-shared" pensions, government should establish or encourage "homemakers' pension credits," which accumulate during the years when a parent is staying home to care for children or elders and not earning an income.

Laws also need to be strengthened to hold parents, especially men, accountable for the care of their children in cases of divorce or childbirth out of wedlock. Some improvements along these lines have been implemented in recent years in connection with welfare-reform policies. In these cases, the cooperation of government with nongovernment institutions is most important because the ability to pay child support and to accept personal responsibility for children cannot be generated simply by government compulsion or by financial incentives or penalties. Employment and a sense of obligation for children must be encouraged in reluctant or troubled parents in a personal way, usually by extended family members and often with the help of faith-based service organizations and churches.

Much progress has been made in recent years—and more still needs to be made—in another area of lawmaking, namely, the crafting of public policies that take into account the fact that employers and employees in the marketplace are also people who may have spouses and children. In other words, while the laws governing business, industry, commerce, and nonprofit employment must be designed to fit these spheres, which are distinguishable from marriage and family life, the law should not treat people as nothing more than market factors. Thus, laws that limit the number of hours in the workday, that protect against sexual discrimination in employment, that foster equal pay for equal work, and that encourage family leave for fathers and mothers after childbirth can help promote justice for women, children, men, and families. They can help make the marketplace an arena in which men and women are not treated unequally when there is no reason for such treatment and in which distinctions can be made for good reasons when they ought to be—for example, in giving particular attention to employees with newborns.

The few instances just cited as examples of public policy considerations are only illustrative. There are dozens of other important areas of public policy—such as health care and health insurance—that bear directly on the health and well-being of families and of the women, men, and children of which they are composed. To these we will need to give our attention as citizens in order to carry forward a Christian contribution to public justice for all our neighbors.

Notes

Chapter 1: The Signs of the Times

1. Nadya Labi, "The Hunter and the Choirboy," *Time* 151, no. 13 (6 April 1998).

Chapter 2: The Rise of Individualism

1. Survey conducted by the Higher Education Research Institute at the University of California, reported on by Leo Reisberg, *The Chronicle of Higher Education* (25 January 1999).

2. Princeton Survey Research Associates, "The Impact of Religious Organizations on Gender Equality: A Report of Findings from a National Survey of Women" (7 January 1999).

3. James Davison Hunter, *Before the Shooting Begins: Searching for Democracy as the Culture Wars Rage* (New York: Free Press, 1994). See also my review of *Before the Shooting Begins* in *First Things* (1994).

4. For a fuller development of this argument, see my forthcoming article in *First Things*.

5. Aristotle said different "in kind"; Locke said "distinct." See Tiffany R. Jones and Larry Peterman, "Whither the Family and Family Privacy?" paper delivered at the annual meeting of the American Political Science Association, Boston, Massachusetts, September 1998, for a discussion of these traditions and developments. The tradition in political theory stretches from Aristotle to John Locke and beyond.

6. For an extended discussion of these issues, see my *Feminism without Illusions: A Critique of Individualism* (Chapel Hill: Univ. of North Carolina Press, 1991); and *"Feminism Is Not the Story of My Life": How the Feminist Elite Has Lost Touch with Women's Real Concerns* (New York: Doubleday, 1996).

7. Jones and Peterman, "Whither the Family?" referring to the views of June Aline Eichbaum, "Towards an Autonomy-Based Theory of Constitutional Privacy: Beyond the Ideology of Familial Privacy," 14 *Harvard Civil Rights and Civil Liberties Law Review* 364 (1979): 381–82; and Anita Allen, *Uneasy Access: Privacy for Women in a Free Society* (Totowa, N.J.: Rowman & Littlefield, 1988), 84–85.

Chapter 3: Feminism and the Struggle for Equality

1. Arlie Hochschild with Anne Machung, *The Second Shift* (New York: Viking, 1989).

2. Mary Ann Glendon, *Rights Talk: The Impoverishment of Political Discourse* (New York: Free Press, 1991).

3. 428 U.S. 52(1976), at 70, cited by Jones and Peterman, "Whither the Family?"

4. Ibid.

5. *Planned Parenthood of Southeastern Pennsylvania v Casey,* 112 Sup. Ct. 2791 (1992).

6. Steven Nock, *Marriage in Men's Lives* (New York: Oxford Univ. Press, 1998).

7. Andrew Cherlin, *Marriage, Divorce, Remarriage,* rev. ed. (Cambridge: Harvard Univ. Press, 1992); and Larry L. Bumpass and James A. Sweet, "Cohabitation, Marriage, and Union Stability: Preliminary Findings from NSFH2," *NSFH Working Paper,* no. 65 (Univ. of Wisconsin-Madison: Center for Demography and Ecology, 1995).

8. Eleanor E. Maccoby, *The Two Sexes* (Cambridge: Harvard Univ. Press, 1998).

9. George A. Akerlof, Janet L. Yellen, and Michael L. Katz, "An Analysis of Out-of-Wedlock Childbearing in the United States," *Quarterly Journal of Economics* CXI (1996): 277–317. It should be noted that Akerlof, Yellen, and Katz write from the liberal rather than the conservative end of the political spectrum. Indeed, President Clinton has recently appointed Janet L. Yellen to the Council of Economic Advisors.

10. George A. Akerlof, "Men without Children," *The Economic Journal* 108 (1998): 287–309.

11. Sara McLanahan and Gary Sandefur, *Growing Up with a Single Parent: What Hurts, What Helps* (Cambridge: Harvard Univ. Press, 1994), 1.

12. Cynthia C. Harper and Sara S. McLanahan, "Father Absence and Youth Incarceration," paper delivered at the annual meeting of the American Sociological Association, San Francisco, 1998; David Popenoe, *Life without Father: Compelling New Evidence That Fatherhood and Marriage Are Indispensable for the Good of Children and Society* (New York: Free Press, 1996); Nicholas Zill and Charlotte A. Schoenborn, "Developmental Learning and Emotional Problems: Health of Our Nation's Children, United States, 1988," *Advance Data,* National Center for Health Statistics, no. 120, 9.

13. Andrew Hacker, "The War over the Family," *New York Review of Books* XLIV, no. 19 (4 December 1997): 36–37.

14. For a fuller discussion of these trends, see Fox-Genovese, *"Feminism Is Not the Story of My Life."* See also Francis Fukuyama, *The Great Disruption: Human Nature and the Disruption of Social Order* (New York: Free Press, 1999).

15. Bumpass and Sweet, "Cohabitation, Marriage, and Union Stability"; and Christopher Ellison, John Bartkowski, and Kristin Anderson, "Are There Religious Variations in Domestic Violence?" *Journal of Family Issues* 20 (1999): 87–113.

16. Danielle Crittenden, *What Our Mothers Didn't Tell Us: Why Happiness Eludes the Modern Woman* (New York: Simon & Schuster, 1999), 110.

Chapter 4: Parents and Children

1. For the sexual and economic revolution, see Fox-Genovese, *"Feminism Is Not the Story of My Life."* See also Fukuyama, *The Great Disruption;* the discussions in Alan Wolfe, "The Shock of the Old," *The New Republic* 4411 (2 August 1999): 42–46;

and David Brooks, "Disruption and Redemption," *Policy Review* 95 (June/July, 1999): 72–77.

2. Wilfred M. McClay, *The Masterless: Self and Society in Modern America* (Chapel Hill: Univ. of North Carolina Press, 1994).

3. Orlando Patterson, *Freedom in the Making of Western Culture* (New York: Basic Books, 1991).

4. Mary Stewart Van Leeuwen, "Re-Inventing the Ties That Bind: Feminism and the Family at the Close of the Twentieth Century," in *Religion, Feminism and the Family,* ed. Anne Carr and Mary Stewart Van Leeuwen (Louisville: Westminster John Knox, 1996), 46. See also Mary Stewart Van Leeuwen et al., *After Eden: Facing the Challenge of Gender Reconciliation* (Grand Rapids: Eerdmans, 1993).

5. Gail Godwin, *The Good Husband* (New York: Ballantine Books, 1994), 465.

Response by Stanley J. Grenz

1. Hence, my book *Sexual Ethics: An Evangelical Perspective,* rev. ed. (Louisville: Westminster John Knox, 1997).

2. John Piper, "A Vision of Biblical Complementarity: Manhood and Womanhood Defined according to the Bible," in *Recovering Biblical Manhood and Womanhood: A Response to Evangelical Feminism,* ed. John Piper and Wayne Grudem (Wheaton: Crossway, 1991), 36, 46.

3. James I. Packer, "Let's Stop Making Women Presbyters," *Christianity Today* (11 February 1991), 20.

4. On this, see for example Kaye Cook and Lance Lee, *Man and Woman: Alone and Together* (Wheaton: Victor/BridgePoint, 1992), 49.

5. Jean Vanier, *Man and Woman He Made Them* (New York: Paulist Press, 1984), 97–98.

6. See, for example, Stephen B. Boyd, *The Men We Long to Be: Beyond Domination to a New Christian Understanding of Manhood* (San Francisco: Harper, 1995), 203.

Response by Mardi Keyes

1. For example, Shulamith Firestone, Simone de Beauvoir, and Alison Jagger.

2. Mary Stewart Van Leeuwen, *Gender and Grace: Love, Work and Parenting in a Changing World* (Downers Grove, Ill.: InterVarsity Press, 1960), 69.

3. Ibid., 70.

4. While women were more vulnerable in the first century than they are in modern America, women, in general, are physically more vulnerable than men in every culture; and in a fallen world, sexist political and socioeconomic structures continue to disadvantage women. Therefore, this text has application in every culture.

5. John Demos, *Past, Present and Personal* (New York: Oxford Univ. Press, 1986), chap. 3.

Response by Mary Stewart Van Leeuwen

1. See in particular Kuyper's *Lectures on Calvinism,* the Stone Foundation Lectures given at Princeton Seminary in 1898 (Grand Rapids: Eerdmans, 1931). For his views on feminism and the roles of women, see especially his *De Eerepositie der*

Vrouw (Kampen: Kok, 1932). For an analysis of this and Kuyper's other writings on gender and family, see Mary Stewart Van Leeuwen, "The Carrot and the Stick: Abraham Kuyper on Gender, Family and Class," in *Religion, Pluralism and Public Life: Abraham Kuyper's Legacy for the 21st Century,* ed. Luis Lugo (Grand Rapids: Eerdmans, forthcoming).

2. Kuyper, *Lectures on Calvinism,* 87, 90–91.

3. Ibid., 91.

4. Ibid.

5. Ibid., 27.

6. Linda Waite, "Does Marriage Matter?" *Demography* 32, no. 4 (November 1995): 483–507; and also her volume *The Case for Marriage* (Cambridge: Harvard Univ. Press, forthcoming).

7. See especially Kuyper's *De Eerepositie der Vrouw,* and for a detailed analysis of same, Mary Stewart Van Leeuwen, "Abraham Kuyper and the Cult of True Womanhood: An Analysis of *De Eerepositie der Vrouw,*" *Calvin Theological Journal* 31, no. 8 (April 1996): 97–124.

8. Kuyper, *De Eerepositie der Vrouw,* 19–20 (English typescript-translation).

9. Ibid., 28.

10. Ibid., 13, 29 (Kuyper's emphasis).

11. Ibid., 29.

12. See in particular Charles Bloomberg, *Christian Nationalism and the Rise of the Afrikaner Broederbond in South Africa, 1918–1948* (Bloomington, Ind.: Indiana Univ. Press, 1989); and John W. DeGruchy and Charles Villa-Vicencio, eds., *Apartheid Is a Heresy* (Grand Rapids: Eerdmans, 1983).

13. For a review of the pertinent empirical studies collected prior to 1970, see Jessie Bernard, *The Future of Marriage* (New York: World Publishers, 1972).

14. As quoted in G. C. Berkhouwer, *Man: The Image of God,* trans. Dirk W. Jellema (Grand Rapids: Eerdmans, 1962), 186. A good example is Kuyper's warning, two decades before the Russian Revolution, that if Christian nations failed to do justice to the poor, God would have to allow some other, apparently godless, movement to take up the task.

15. For a more detailed outline, see Neil Gilbert, "Working Families: Hearth to Market," in *All Our Families: New Policies for a New Century,* ed. Mary Ann Amson, Arlene Skolnick, and Stephen Sugarman (New York: Oxford Univ. Press, 1998), 193–216; and for a practical-theological elaboration, see Mary Stewart Van Leeuwen, "Faith, Feminism and Family in an Age of Globalization," in *Religion, Globalization and the Spheres of Life: Theological Ethics in a Pluralistic World,* ed. Max Stackhouse, Peter Paris, and Diane Obenchain, 4 vols. (Harrisburg, Pa.: Trinity Press International, forthcoming).

16. Mary Stewart Van Leeuwen, "What Are the Most Pressing Issues Today in Relations between Men and Women? Crucial Steps Needed to Help Bind Families," *The Chronicle of Higher Education* 45, no. 6 (2 October 1998): B-8.

Elizabeth Fox-Genovese is Eleonore Raoul Professor of the Humanities at Emory University in Atlanta, where she also directed the Women's Studies program from 1986 to 1991. A graduate of Bryn Mawr College, she studied in Paris for a year before pursuing her doctoral studies at Harvard (Ph.D., 1974). She won the Holman Prize from the Society for the Study of Southern Literature for her 1988 book, *Within the Plantation Household: Black and White Women of the Old South* (Univ. of North Carolina Press). She is also the author of *"Feminism Is Not the Story of My Life": How Today's Feminist Elite Has Lost Touch with the Real Concerns of Women* (Doubleday, 1996). Her scholarship and writings cover topics ranging from feminism and the family to sexual harassment, from slavery to multiculturalism.